To Judith Clayton
With all good wishes —
William A. Banner

Moral Norms and Moral Order

Moral Norms and Moral Order

The Philosophy of Human Affairs

William Augustus Banner

A University of Florida Book
University Presses of Florida
Gainesville

University Presses of Florida is the central agency for scholarly publishing of the State of Florida's university system. Its offices are located at 15 NW 15th Street, Gainesville, FL 32603. Works published by University Presses of Florida are evaluated and selected for publication by a faculty editorial committee of any one of Florida's nine public universities: Florida A&M University (Tallahassee), Florida Atlantic University (Boca Raton), Florida International University (Miami), Florida State University (Tallahassee), University of Central Florida (Orlando), University of Florida (Gainesville), University of North Florida (Jacksonville), University of South Florida (Tampa), University of West Florida (Pensacola).

Library of Congress Cataloging in Publication Data

Banner, William Augustus.
Moral norms and moral order.

"A University of Florida book."
Includes bibliographical references and index.
1. Ethics. I. Title.
BJ1012.B363 170 80-24206
ISBN 0-8130-0661-9

PRINTED IN USA

To Beatrice, Anne, and Perry

Is Justice . . . variable or mutable? No; but the times, rather, which Justice governs, are not like one another; for they are times.

St. Augustine, *The Confessions*, III, vii

Contents

Preface

ARISTOTLE, in the concluding section of the *Nicomachean Ethics,* speaks of his ethical theory as the *philosophy of human affairs* (ἡ περὶ τὰ ἀνθρώπινα φιλοσοφία). In summarizing his lengthy treatment of moral questions, Aristotle is satisfied that adequate discussion has been given to happiness and virtue and to friendship and pleasure as intrinsic goods. He recognizes at the same time that virtue is something to be practiced as well as possessed, and that attention must be given to the ways in which the practice of virtue, which is always difficult, can be supported against the allurement of passion. This brings Aristotle to speak of the function of law and public regulation in the nurture of the good man, a matter to be pursued in a separate treatise on politics. While there are individual writings on ethics and politics, it is clear that Aristotle thought of the two investigations as having the same task, namely, the elucidation of moral nobility and justice (*τὰ δὲ καλὰ καὶ τὰ δίκαια*).

This book has been written in agreement with Aristotle's inclusive view of human affairs as a subject embracing, as one whole, matters that today would be regarded as properly treated under separate headings of ethics, politics, and law. Distinctions introduced into a complex subject matter are useful, particularly in enabling a careful and tidy consideration of compartmentalized problems. But such distinctions need not be allowed to break up a genuine unity of experience and meaning. Human existence being naturally social, the moral life has the unity of the norm or norms that govern at once both personal and public affairs. What an individual determines to make of his life is of course a personal matter; in carrying out this effort, what an individual requires of resources not his own is a public matter. Both the personal and the public pertain to the quality of individual life. The concerns of individuals as citizens involve simply the translation of human aspiration into public policies, which prescribe the duties of organized effort. Political life is the activity of persons in the collective pursuit of individual well-being. Ethics and politics are thus concerned with the same realm of existence and with the same principal notions, namely, the good, the right, and the just.

Aristotle speaks of law as a rule of reason that has compulsory force. This view of law as rational moral governance, directed to the common good, has been opposed by the general argument that law is independent of morality and that law is validated by its own norm of *legitimacy.* Despite the pretensions of its advocates to present only what is cogent and rigorous, the latter position is clearly incompatible not only with the recognition of the rights of persons but also with the recognition that the means of control and coercion must be such as reasonable individuals would devise in their own interest.

One of the most perplexing problems of morality is the treatment of individuals who inflict injury upon others. In respect for the rights of persons, attention must be given to wrongdoing and to punishment as accountability for wrongdoing. The moral ordering of punishment has for a long time been hampered by confusions concerning the power of society or of the state over its members, particularly those members who are identified as wrongdoers. It is the task of ethical discussion, in correction of these confusions, to reach a determination of punishment that is in conformity with what is both fair and humane. What is defended in these pages is the idea of punishment as restoration or restitution, as an alternative to the theories of retaliation (counter-suffering), correction, and deterrence.

On public questions in general, this book presents an alternative to two positions that have had wide influence in the contemporary world, namely, legal positivism and utilitarianism. It is believed, on the one side, that the concern of the legal positivist is too narrow to treat adequately of pressing social questions, inasmuch as the positivist's attention is given to the consideration of 'law' or 'social policy' *as it is.* Such a consideration subtracts from the character of justice as a moral norm that embraces the guarantees that citizens owe to one another in the imposition of compensation for injuries, in the exchange of goods and services, and in the preservation of the social order itself.

One finds, on the other side, that the views of the utilitarian are too vague to provide a basis for an order of 'reciprocal freedom' or for the reform of an existing order where freedom does not obtain. Utilitarianism, in a word, sets forth the maximizing of good (as pleasure, satisfaction, enjoyment, 'true good for the world as a whole') as the social end to be sought, just as it sets forth 'conduciveness to good' as the standard by which conduct is to be appraised as right or wrong. While one can hardly quarrel with the idea of enlightened interest directed toward maximum human felicity, one looks in vain for the *pattern* of good or goods to be generated for 'the greatest number' through action guided by benevolence. It is chiefly with respect to the *content* of justice that utilitarian ideas about the promotion of human good are disappointing, a weakness of utilitarianism more apparent in some writers than in others.

It is recognized that the issues discussed in this book are broad and difficult. It is intended that the treatment of these matters will contribute to the resolution of some difficulties. The question at bottom is that of the rights and duties of the individual in an organized society. If it is not tolerable for individuals in society to have simply what they wish or to do simply as they please, it is important and necessary to know what one is justified in having without depriving others and what one can do without injuring others.

There is always the hope that what one has written will find acceptance, especially with those individuals who have been one's mentors over a period of many years. A work worthy of such acceptance would settle in some measure a debt to persons whose qualities of mind and spirit exemplified a pattern of "plain living and high thinking" and affirmed the greatness and usefulness of teaching. Beyond this, I wish to say a word of thanks to the editors of University Presses of Florida for their consideration and helpfulness. To my wife, Beatrice, I express my gratitude for support in this task as in all other things.

Washington, D. C. / January, 1980 *W. A. B.*

1 *Moral Norms and Human Affairs*

Norm and Practice

A *norm* is a canon, or standard, of measure or estimation. The *carpenter's norm* is a fixed device for ascertaining an angle of ninety degrees. The norm of the carpenter, as a device, must be said to indicate rather than to establish what in carpentry is taken to be 'square', or 'true'. One is not likely to say that the 'rightness' of the carpenter's joint derives from the rightness or right use of the carpenter's rule. Rather, one would say that the norm represents what is indeed a right angle as distinct from any and all appearances of rightness which may mislead the carpenter in his work. A right angle is simply what it is, and the carpenter's norm exhibits for the practical purposes of carpentry what a right angle is just as a correct map exhibits the contour of the land or the contour of the road. Similarly, a *moral norm* is a standard by which human activity and action can be judged to be approximations in one degree or another to what is *actual.*

There are, of course, many uses of the term 'norm' which do not appear to enjoy the simplicity and straightforwardness of *coincidence* with what obtains independently as the actual. In many cases, in speaking of norms of human behavior, it would appear that the norm *does* establish rather than indicate what is optimum in possibility. It is perhaps in this respect that one thinks of a norm such as 'the representative firm' or 'the representative college'. A firm may be representative simply as the firm whose business practices or merchandising techniques have dominated in a certain trade and have been imitated by other firms in the same trade and in other trades. One may imagine that other firms might have set themselves up or been accepted as 'representative' institutions under other circumstances or in other situations. Thus the status of the representative firm as a 'norm' would seem to indicate nothing beyond the process or processes by which performance or success or prominence was made possible. And it would be believed, accordingly, that there is no 'correct' or 'actual' way (in the normative sense) of doing business that the representative firm models,[1] just as there is no correct or actual way of teaching that the representative college exemplifies.

This view may well be extended to the whole of human affairs, so as to maintain that there is no correct or optimal way of doing anything. Such presumably was the position on human affairs of the ancient Sophists, who gave attention to how it is, as social or political process, that moral and legal norms are established and overthrown. On this view, of course, normative considerations are merely part of the considerations of the mechanics of success and power.[2]

One may, however, go beyond the description of how any given practice came to exist and to prevail and argue that in some way 'the representative firm' does exhibit 'correctness' or

1. Cf. Neill W. Chamberlain, *The Firm: Micro-Economic Planning and Action* (New York: McGraw-Hill Book Company, 1962), p. 407: "There is no 'logically objective' standard by which a company may judge itself. . . . Even after making . . . comparisons, it has no basis for asserting that its performance (or that of any of its reference companies) is good or poor in a definitive sense. It has no way of determining a theoretical or hypothetical standard of excellence with which it may compare itself. . . . Experience constitutes the only basis for judging the quality of performance, and the use of experience as a guide necessitates comparison with others, and with one's own past."

2. Cf. W. K. C. Guthrie, *The Sophists* (Cambridge: Cambridge University Press, 1971), pp. 27-54, 164-75.

completeness of economic operation as the carpenter's rule exhibits the 'rightness' of the right angle. Such correctness would obtain in what may be referred to as "efficiency of operation," "reliability of product," "reliability of service," or "integrity of contract." And the suggestion would be that such correctness should obtain for any firm or enterprise coming forward to provide certain goods or services. The representative firm would indicate, accordingly, what is actual or excellent in human activity rather than reflect merely the energies of resourceful and clever entrepreneurs.

If one follows this approach in human affairs, one would be concerned not with the *how* of human practice but with the *wherefore*. One would want to know on what basis a given practice is commended as 'good practice'. One would ask, for example, what case can be made for the relationship that obtained between lords and serfs under manorial tenure, the condition of serfs being described as follows:

> . . . their characteristic disabilities were first, their absence of right of appeal to the king for justice, and second, their absence of right over their own chattels and holdings. Both disabilities made them helpless victims of fiscal exploitation. A lord could tallage his villeins at his will: he could exact fines from them, by reason of their unfreedom.[3]

Doubtless a close knowledge of social conditions and social exigencies would inform us as to certain causes or occasions of

3. Marion Gibbs, *Feudal Order* (New York: Henry Schuman, 1963), pp. 90-91. Cf. Walter Ullman, *The Individual and Society in the Middle Ages* (Baltimore: The Johns Hopkins Press, 1966), pp. 15, 17: "The inequality of the members of society showed itself most manifestly in the unequal treatment before the law, for the superior was treated differently from an inferior. . . . subjects were not entitled to invoke the help of a law court against a superior. . . . those members of society who had no office not only stood at the very bottom of the social ladder but also were without public rights. The individual's standing within society was based upon his office or his official function: the greater it was, the more scope it had, the weightier it was, the more rights the individual had. As a mere subject the individual was no more than a recipient of orders, of commands, of the law. . . ."

the practices of manorial tenure. It may be argued, accordingly, that always some fact or facts of origin must be accepted as the reason or reasons for the emergence of a rule or practice, and that knowledge of such fact or facts of origin is the only empirical index of the 'good sense' or 'soundness' of a rule or practice. But to be satisfied with this would be to allow that in a given context there can be only one conceivable mode of life or manner of conduct in support of some interest or in satisfaction of some need. And this would be tantamount to saying that, in a given situation, a particular direction in human affairs can never be a mistake. What would be ignored, of course, is the possibility that the prevailing rule or practice owes its being to contingencies of decision and action that actually favored the 'worse' practice over the 'better'. One can recognize that a prevailing rule or practice, as an ordering, is a social or political phenomenon having a particular social or political genesis; one can also recognize that a rule or practice, when viewed as one among many possible orderings, involves a moral claim which requires justification through moral intuition or moral argument.[4]

It is seen, accordingly, that the moral consideration of a rule or practice involves a consideration of end as well as means, that is, a consideration of what is fitting and preferable as a human condition for all individuals to whom the rule or practice applies. A rule as an ordering is always an ordering of a particular something; that is, an ordering supporting some specific end or ends rather than others and employing some partic-

4. Cf. William James, *The Principles of Psychology* (New York: Henry Holt and Company, 1918), 2:672: "The *moral* principles which our mental structure engenders are quite as little explicable *in toto* by habitual experiences having bred inner cohesions. Rightness is not *mere* usualness, wrongness not *mere* oddity, however numerous the facts which might be invoked to prove such identity. Nor are the moral judgments those most invariably and emphatically impressed on us by public opinion. The most characteristically and peculiarly moral judgments that a man is ever called on to make are in unprecedented cases and lonely emergencies, where no popular rhetorical maxims can avail, and the hidden oracle alone can speak; and it speaks often in favor of conduct quite unusual, and suicidal as far as gaining popular approbation goes."

ular means rather than others to this end or ends. 'Order' and 'what is ordered' are distinguishable although inseparable things, and one need not allow that any order whatsoever is better than anarchy. *What is ordered* is a content that must be appraised in terms of what is beneficial or harmful to particular individuals or to individuals as members of a particular group or class.

It is in considering the 'wherefore' rather than the 'how' of any given rule or practice that one is able to see that a rule cannot by its mere existence establish a norm in the moral sense. A rule that is 'in effect' has only the status of what is operative, that is, the status of 'what is made to work' through sanctions of one sort or another. Of course, the student of society or of law and government can confine himself to the treatment of a rule as merely what is commanded or ordered, and he can maintain, accordingly, that any presumed moral deficiency of the rule does not affect its status and validity as something that is to be obeyed. But this does not mean, as it has been believed by some, that moral justification is extraneous to the consideration of the validity of the rule.[5] A rule may deserve to be disobeyed and the reasons for such disobedience would presumably be forthcoming.

It is not at all instructive to say that a rule as social or legal fact is something to be obeyed. The power or sanction that enjoins obedience to a rule is really extrinsic to the rule itself. What is often involved in talk about 'obedience' is a convenient shift from *what is to be obeyed* (that is, what is ordered or commanded) to *obeying* as the act of conforming to a 'valid' law or rule. When Hans Kelsen, for example, speaks of the *Grundnorm* as the standard that sets up and authorizes valid rules,[6] he is speaking of the elemental competence and effectiveness that elicit obedience but do not provide, in moral terms at least, justification for obedience. Kelsen, then, is really confusing the issue in obtruding matters of efficacy and sanction upon the consideration of matters of justice and fairness, under the guise of freeing the treatment of law and justice from

5. Cf. Hans Kelsen, *Reine Rechtslehre* (Vienna, 1960), pp. 67-71.
6. Kelsen, *Reine Rechtslehre*, p. 197.

extraneous moral concerns. But if 'law' is always an 'ordering' (as an arranging of means with respect to ends), the situation is really the reverse as regards what is extraneous. And one must say, then, that the concerns of the legal scientist or legal positivist rather than the concerns of the moral philosopher are peripheral if not alien to the determination of the *validity* of rules and practices in a society.[7]

Reason and Sentiment in Morals

It is not uncommon in situations of conflict of interests to appeal to what is a reasonable end to pursue or what is the reasonable thing to do. This suggests that there is an appraisal of purposes and a determination of the good and the right that are independent of attitude and passion. This suggests also that two or more individuals can recognize what is *reasonable* as the genuine expression of their interests, if only after a long and difficult process of discussion and debate. Bishop Butler, in the eighteenth century, called attention to the place of reflection in the moral life:

> There is a principle of reflection in men, by which they distinguish between, approve and disapprove their own actions. We are plainly constituted such creatures as to reflect upon our own nature. The mind can take a view of what passes within itself, its propensions, aversions, passions, affections, as respecting such objects, and in such degrees; and of the several actions consequent thereupon. . . . And that this faculty tends to restrain men from doing mischief to each other, and leads them to do good, is too manifest to need being insisted upon. . . . It is needless to compare the respect [the principle of reflection] has to private good, with the respect it has to public good; since it plainly tends as much to the latter as to the former, and is commonly thought to tend chiefly to the latter.[8]

7. Cf. Gustav Radbruch, *Rechtsphilosophie*, 6th ed. (Stuttgart: K. F. Koehler, 1963), pp. 180-83.

8. Joseph Butler, *Sermons on Human Nature*, no. 1, in *British Moralists*, ed. L. A. Selby-Bigge (Indianapolis: The Bobbs-Merrill Company, Inc., 1964), 1:201-2.

Butler affirms the capacity of reason to indicate "how liable we are to be led wrong by passion and private interest" and he goes on to speak of the bearing of "reasonable good-will, and the right behavior toward our fellow-creatures" upon the attainment of the greatest public good.[9] One is aware, of course, that many social and legal scientists would be quick to say that it is precisely the lack of agreement as to what is 'reasonable' in behavior and the lack of hope of reaching agreement through moral reflection that have inspired and supported efforts to free all discussion of public rules from considerations of rightness and wrongness, of justice and injustice. And these social and legal scientists would be joined by many moral philosophers. As a matter of fact, the situation in moral philosophy involves much more than attention to the variation and relativity of moral judgment. Contemporary moralists in impressive numbers have adopted a skeptical posture, holding that moral judgment in the very nature of the case cannot be cognitive.

Recent theories of moral valuation that have been influenced by psychological and sociological analyses and 'findings' have, on the one side, represented moral norms (and all moral predicates such as 'good' and 'right') as projections of interests, feelings, and attitudes peculiar to the individual or to groups of individuals. This is the development that has come to be known as *ethical naturalism.*[10] On the other side are the views of those who have wished to avoid the somewhat harsh position of the naturalists and to hold that there is something distinctly *ethical* about moral judgments. The latter theorists have wished to maintain, at the same time, that moral judgments are ascriptive rather than cognitive.[11] Thus one is left with a choice between the naturalists who insist that the moralist must speak as a behavioral scientist and those noncognitivists who concede

9. Butler, *Sermons on Human Nature,* no. 12, in *British Moralists,* 1:241-42.

10. Cf. C. D. Broad, *Five Types of Ethical Theory* (London: Routledge and Kegan Paul, Ltd., 1951), pp. 259-64. See also A. C. Ewing, *The Definition of Good* (New York: The Macmillan Company, 1947), pp. 36-77.

11. Cf. George C. Kerner, *The Revolution in Ethical Theory* (New York: Oxford University Press, 1966), pp. 40-96.

that the moralist can speak as a moralist inasmuch as he wishes only to inform us of his moral feelings or dispositions and perhaps to move us to feel as he does.

It should be clear that it is impossible to inquire about the correctness of rules and practices if the only accessible 'norms' are those involved or associated with the interests and tastes of individuals or groups of individuals. If moral judgment cannot stand as an independent reckoning of what is good or right, then prevailing practice as the expression of what certain individuals find pleasing or advantageous must be accepted as the only real program of human affairs—and for as long as these individuals find such practice to be to their pleasure or advantage. One must say, then, either that the ethical is a domain of cognition and truth or that the conduct of human affairs is arbitrary and beyond discussion. And if the latter, then morality (as justice) is indeed the advantage of the stronger individual.

It is doubtful, however, that anyone concerned about his interests in contest with the interests of others is prepared to accept the elimination of reflection and debate from the realm of morals. The situations in which individuals find themselves, at any given time, are either better or worse for such individuals than recognizable or conceivable alternatives. It would be a tedious evasion of the most immediate issues of human life to contend, for example, that an individual's views about 'freedom' are without public significance in the defense of *his* freedom against his unfreedom.

A discussion concerning moral alternatives is a genuine discussion or debate about human situations, even if one should grant that the alternatives are, in some respects at least, involved with expressions of feeling and attitude. In giving attention to the affective accompaniments of moral judgments, there is always the temptation to think that such judgments are merely or largely subjective, that is, that they are peculiar to one individual or another and indicative of moral dispositions rather than moral situations. But one must be reminded that a judgment is always *about* something which is discriminable through the terms of the judgment. Where forms of speech are joined in declarative sentences, there is an involvement through language in a common world of assertion and designation in agreement or disagreement with other individuals. Anything which can be mentioned can become a matter of discussion within the rules of grammar and logic. It is certainly not apparent that we cannot speak clearly and critically in moral terms about persons, about the dignity of persons, and about the rights and duties of persons in society as we speak clearly and critically in appropriate terms about other subjects.

Morality and Public Policy

It would seem that it is necessary above all to bring public policy and practice and moral judgment and analysis together in the same forum. What is ordered under public policy has a moral content that is separable from its imperative expression. To declare the policy 'Loitering is forbidden' and then to enforce it is to deny to some persons what they may well take to be pleasant and advantageous behavior. Under this ordering, the individual who is bent upon loitering is either mistaken about his own advantage or he is being prevented from pursuing what is indeed good. The proscription of loitering thus raises substantive moral questions concerning what is good and what is or is not a claim of the individual upon the social resources of freedom.

One recognizes, accordingly, that public policy, as a norm which is valid for persons as members of a community, is more than public quiet. The confusion between public quiet and good order is a constant threat to the freedom of the individual. Aristotle has made the point that public policy depends for its content and authority upon what is morally justifiable. The purpose of the laws, in agreement with the conclusions of ethics, is to make people better. Social authority can do what the individual cannot always do on his own behalf, namely, support and maintain good habits in the face of the dispositions to passion and indulgence.[12] Legislation—that is, just law—is a moral instrument that embraces the two elements

12. Aristotle, *Nicomachean Ethics*, 10. 9. 6-9.

of compulsive power and right order. Law, in its essential character or ethical pretension, is a rule of reason, "a rule proceeding from a sort of practical reason or wisdom."[13]

The view of Aristotle, namely, that the foundation and validity of just law lie within moral philosophy, stands opposed in recent times by theories that have affirmed the separation of law from morals, either explicitly as in the legal positivism of Hans Kelsen[14] or implicitly as in the ethical relativism of Gustav Radbruch. The intellectual career of Radbruch is in many ways illustrative of the dimensions of the modern conflict between morality and law. In his important work, *Rechtsphilosophie,* published first in 1914, Radbruch expressed the view that the correctness of "ultimate ought statements" (*letzten Sollenssätze*) cannot be established and that there can be no rational decision between opposing value propositions.[15] While in the ordering of means to ends law does have an ethical content, this content cannot be justified through rational argument. Ethical relativism is inescapable inasmuch as the relativity of moral judgment is irresolvable. In later writings, published between 1945 and 1949, Radbruch repudiated his earlier relativism, observing that this position left the legal theorist defenseless against arbitrary and in some cases criminal enactment.[16]

There is clearly a continuing need for the exposition and application of moral rules that are regulative of the whole of human affairs. In the modern world we have had the distinc-

13. Aristotle, *Nicomachean Ethics*, 10. 9. 12.

14. Cf. Kelsen, *Reine Rechtslehre*, pp. 65-69.

15. Radbruch, *Rechtsphilosophie*, pp. 102-3: "Die hier dargelegte Methode nennt sich *Relativismus,* weil sie die Richtigkeit jedes Werturteils nur in Beziehung zu einem bestimmten obersten Werturteil, nur in Rahmen einer bestimmten Wert- und Weltanschauung, nicht aber die Richtigkeit dieses Werturteils, dieser Wert- und Weltanschauung selbst festzustellen sich zur Aufgabe macht."

16. Radbruch, *Rechtsphilosophie,* appendix, pp. 352-53: "Der Positivismus hat in der Tat mit seiner Ueberzeugung 'Gesetz ist Gesetz' den deutschen Juristenstand wehrlos gemacht gegen Gesetze willkürlichen und verbrecherischen Inhalts. . . . Denn man kann Recht, auch positives Recht, gar nicht anders definieren denn als eine Ordnung und Satzung, die ihrem Sinn nach bestimmt ist, der Gerechtigkeit zu dienen."

tion, within the public realm, of autonomous departments of activity, each with its own 'canons' of 'correctness'. With advances in commerce and industry, for example, has come the projection of economic 'laws' which purport to express the mechanisms of wealth-getting quite apart from any moral norms governing the acquisition and distribution of divisible goods. With the rise of the modern state has come the projection of ideas of the legitimacy of the prevailing order and of the validity of its rules or laws, quite apart from or in disregard of the natural rights of the governed.

One consequence of these developments has been the reduction of moral norms to self-justifying interests of one sort or another. One encounters a crisis in value, inasmuch as there remains no way of appraising particular interests apart from their vitality and force and the viability of the operations that the pursuit of such interests entails. Such a crisis in value involves a crisis in culture, as there is no way of determining what is better or worse, as social policy, for the members of society as a whole. If moral analysis leads only to the discrimination of self-justifying interests, there is obviously no place for the common assessment of the objects of interest, with respect to their worth and their subordination one to another in a hierarchy of intrinsic and instrumental goods.

What is required is an ontology of morals,[17] in the sense of an affirmation of human values as realities, or actualities, that are the ground rather than the reflection of interests and attitudes. Moral philosophy, as distinct from social science, must encompass the pattern of human striving in relation to the pattern of human well-being as *being.* The many dimensions of human activity must be viewed under norms that set forth what an individual can become as a complete being in a community of peers. The technical or compartmental considerations of human affairs, as matters of interest to the social scientist, concern merely the operations that apply precise means to ends. Moral considerations, on the other hand, pertain to the

17. For this expression, I am indebted, in recent literature, to Henry B. Veatch's book, *For an Ontology of Morals* (Evanston: Northwestern University Press, 1971).

validity or justification of the ends themselves and to the adequacy or fitness of the means committed thereto. It is to exploration of the *realm* of morals, particularly in elucidation of the relation of moral nobility to justice, that the following chapters are devoted.

2 *The Good*

The Notion of Good

Aristotle observed in the ancient world that the term 'good' is used in many senses in accordance with the many kinds of things that are distinguished as good.[1] The diversity of good things clearly defies a very useful grouping of goods as *intrinsic* and *instrumental,* inasmuch as many things that are sought for their own sake (such as honor, wisdom, and pleasure) are really distinct and not of the same kind. What Aristotle proposes in a passing remark is that diverse things have in common a relationship, as good, to differing things, that is, as sight is good in the body, so intelligence is good in the soul.[2] Thus, by an analogy of proportionality, diversity is embraced under common meaning and usage. Although univocal meaning cannot be achieved, the disaster of equivocal meaning is avoided.

Aristotle offers yet another clue to the meaning and use of the term 'good' in defining the good as that at which all things aim (*τἀγαθὸν οὗ πάντ' ἐφίεται*) or that for the sake of

1. Aristotle, *Nicomachean Ethics,* 1. 6. 3.
2. Aristotle, *Nicomachean Ethics,* 1. 6. 12.

which everything else is done (οὗ χάριν τὰ λοιπὰ πράττεται). Aristotle is apparently thinking of the sense in which, in common usage, 'good' as a term indicates the completion of the natural tendency of a thing or the completion of the purpose of some instrument or device. Such a locution defines 'good' but not in the sense of exposing the genus to which goodness belongs and the differentia by which goodness is distinguished from other species of the same genus. This is because good is not a kind of thing as *horse* or *man* is a kind of thing, or a highest kind (category) such as substance or quality. If many diverse things are good, as Aristotle holds in agreement with common sense, then 'good' or 'goodness' is compatible with these things (with pleasure and virtue, for example) without being essentially what these things are. This can be so only if *good* is an attribute of being as a supervenient quality and is not *being* itself or a kind of being.

It is not surprising, therefore, that Aristotle, in trying to indicate what 'good' is, comes around one way or another to analogies drawn from the arts (τέχναι). Wherever there is completion, Aristotle is prepared to recognize goodness; and, accordingly, where there is aiming (ἐφίεσθαι), what is 'aimed at' is recognizable as good. Every art, whether medicine, strategy, or harp playing, aims at some precise end, namely, health, victory in combat, or excellence in harp playing itself. The teleology of the arts becomes for Aristotle an analogue of the teleology of existence itself, particularly where the good is precisely human good and indeed good within human reach.[3] The clue to man's good is the aiming of man, that is, of the individual. The moral philosopher must simply carry out the job of analysis in order to discover the intention or thrust of human existing, its aiming toward completion or excellence, as one discovers the thrust or aiming of the harp player.

In not considering 'good' as a biologist would consider and classify a living thing, Aristotle makes an approach to the nature of good to which many objections can be raised. It may be said, for example, that Aristotle really confuses 'good' with

3. Aristotle, *Nicomachean Ethics,* 1. 6. 13.

'being' and in so doing really reduces good to being and thus commits in his own way what G. E. Moore has called the *naturalistic fallacy.*[4] The question here is whether 'good' when considered in terms of completion or fulfillment becomes interchangeable with 'being'. In a certain sense this is so, inasmuch as the virtuous, or good, man for Aristotle is one who has reached his *entelechy,* that is, his final form or full being. But in a more strict sense, 'good' is not interchangeable with 'being'. The virtuous man is not naturally good: a man can *be* without being a good man, as there can be harp playing without excellence of harp playing. Whereas one cannot think of what was completed without thinking of what was to be completed, one can certainly think of *what is occurring* without thinking of *what is being completed.*

With Aristotle, the term 'good' is applied to being which is *actual* and designates, at least in man and in other living things, activities of completeness (*ἐνέργεια τοῦ τετελεσμένου*), which are accordingly unhindered activities (*ἐνέργειαι ἀνεμπόδιστοι*).[5] The use of 'good' in this sense is not trivial or redundant, inasmuch as completion may be frustrated if a thing is diverted by circumstances from the full exercise of its powers and from such satisfaction as accompanies the full exercise of its powers.[6] If 'good' is interchangeable with 'being', it is only so with 'being' in the normative sense, that is, with 'being' in the sense of 'actual'. It is in this sense of 'what ought to be' that 'good' as a term designates the norm or norms that are discovered or discoverable in the nature of things. And thus it is as inquiry directed to such discovery that ethics or moral philosophy has a foundation as a normative science, a science of discoverable norms of human activity and action.

As observed earlier, one stumbling block of modern ethical discussion has been the recognition of and preoccupation with the psychological circumstances that attend the use of moral terms. The occasions of the use of the term 'good' are also

4. G. E. Moore, *Principia Ethica* (Cambridge: Cambridge University Press, 1954), p. 176.

5. Aristotle, *Nicomachean Ethics,* 7. 13. 2.

6. Aristotle, *Nicomachean Ethics,* 10. 4. 5.

occasions of the involvement of the individual with interests (desires) and affections (feelings). This involvement may be taken to suggest that the use of 'good' is only brought about by experiences of excitement and feeling as precise dispositions of particular individuals. Moral investigation may be thought, then, to begin and end with the investigation of excitement and feeling as part of the study of consciousness itself, which we know as psychological inquiry.

It should be clear that the restriction of the meaning of moral terms to the expression of excitement and feeling is tantamount to the elimination of ethical discussion and the cancellation of ethical problems. For it is evident that all interests and affections, as data of consciousness, are equally genuine—if not equally fascinating to the student of human behavior. Moral distinctions such as 'good' and 'bad', as used only in the articulation of experiences of desiring and feeling, could involve nothing more than a verbal game, which individuals carry on within themselves or carry on outside of themselves in seeking to delight, offend, or otherwise move other individuals. Any attempt to speak of an 'object' of desire or feeling as a good or bad object would be inconsistent or incompatible with the restriction of the 'realm' of morals to excitements and affections,[7] as would also be any attempt to resolve conflicts of 'view' about things taken to be 'good' and 'bad'.

It is true, of course, that the individual often reports his experience as though there are moral distinctions *within* consciousness, as in speaking of feelings of pride and shame. But clearly the attention here is to something other than consciousness itself; it is to the referent or referents of consciousness.[8]

7. Cf. Thomas Hobbes, *Leviathan*, ed. Michael Oakeshott (Oxford: Basil Blackwell, 1960), chap. 6, pp. 32-33: ". . . these words of good, evil, and contemptible, are ever used with relation to the person that useth them: there being nothing simply and absolutely so; nor any common rule of good and evil, to be taken from the nature of the objects themselves; but from the person of the man, where there is no commonwealth; or, in a commonwealth, from the person that representeth it; or from an arbitrator or judge, whom men disagreeing shall by consent set up, and make his sentence the rule thereof."

8. Cf. R. B. Perry, *Realms of Value* (Cambridge, Mass.: Harvard Uni-

The normative character that Hume accords to the moral feelings (for example, sympathy[9]) and that J. S. Mill accords to the "conscientious feelings"[10] really involves the *objects* of these affections as these objects are responded to and approved by the individual.

It must be said, accordingly, that ethical investigation in its attention to *what* is desired or approved is not merely verbal but involves the consideration of the *character* of the things that are taken to be good.[11] This can be said simply because the presumption in the use of the term 'good' is the recognition of something that is good, as in speaking of the good harp player or the good citizen. Whether the harp player or the citizen is indeed *good* can be determined only through the clear sense of what goodness is or of what is required for anything to be recognized as good. The responses that are aroused by or associated with good things are themselves distinguishable from such good things, as any response is necessarily distinguishable from that to which it is a response. Thus it is that the language of moral designation cannot be reduced to the language of

---

versity Press, 1954), p. 122: "The datum of feeling may be taken to signify the state or act of feeling; or it may be taken to signify what is felt. . . . in the second case, it is the object of the feeling which is observed, and the feeling is the observing."

9. Cf. David Hume, *A Treatise of Human Nature,* ed. L. A. Selby-Bigge (Oxford: The Clarendon Press, 1958), bk. 3, pt. 3, sec. 1, pp. 577-78: ". . . it appears, *that* sympathy is a very powerful principle in human nature, *that* it has a great influence on our taste of beauty, and *that* it produces our sentiment of morals in all the artificial virtues. From thence we may presume, that it also gives rise to many of the other virtues; and that qualities acquire our approbation, because of their tendency to the good of mankind. This presumption must become a certainty, when we find that most of those qualities which we *naturally* approve of, have actually that tendency, and render a man a proper member of society. . . ."

10. Cf. J. S. Mill, *Utilitarianism,* chap. 3, in *The Utilitarians* (Garden City, N.Y.: Dolphin Books, 1961), pp. 432-33.

11. Cf. R. M. Hare, *Freedom and Reason* (Oxford: The Clarendon Press, 1963), p. 23: ". . . typical moral disputes are not purely verbal, as on a naturalist account they would be, provided the non-verbal facts were agreed."

moral disposition. The point here is that the intention, in the use of the term 'good', must be what exists as good or appears to be good. The term 'good', in its use or application, is simply more pervasive than most common terms and is predicated in all of the categories or kinds of being.

Intrinsic Good and the Useful

The recognition that the term 'good' is used in many senses may prompt one to prepare a lexicon of uses that will be both precise and exhaustive.[12] At the same time, one may be prompted to give attention to what would be considered the primary use of 'good', upon which all other uses of the term depend. While Aristotle proposes that many things are called good "by way of a proportion," he also proposes that some things are called good in that "they all contribute to one good."[13] And with respect to the latter proposal, Aristotle considers the utility of the distinction between things good for their own sake (intrinsic goods) and things good for the sake of other things (instrumental goods). One sees, of course, that this distinction gives trouble, not only because intrinsic goods turn out to be of many kinds but also because a thing may at one time be regarded as an intrinsic good and at another time as an instrumental good. One thinks here of such a thing as a book of poetry which is prized for its own sake but which may at times be useful as a paperweight on one's desk or as an item in exchange for another book of poetry.

Nevertheless, there is warrant for the priority of intrinsic good over instrumental good. The prizing of the surgeon's scalpel is inferior to the prizing of the surgeon's skill, as the prizing of the skill of healing is inferior to the prizing of health itself. There are, as a matter of fact, things such as health and pleasure that are prized and sought for their own sake, whereas there are other things that are sought merely as instruments to the production or maintenance of things sought for their own sake. There is a distinction to be made, in any means-to-end relation-

12. Cf. Georg Henrik von Wright, *The Varieties of Goodness* (London: Routledge and Kegan Paul, Ltd., 1963), pp. 8-18.

13. Aristotle, *Nicomachean Ethics,* 1. 6. 12.

ship, between the useful and that with respect to which something is useful. One can, accordingly, think of a good such as pleasure that is supported by one or many things but that itself is not instrumental to anything.

There is, however, the problem of determining in what precise way the goodness of what is useful differs from the goodness of what is prized or esteemed for its own sake. It may be thought that what is intrinsically good is indeed *good* whereas what is useful is ethically neutral until some use is made of it. The value neutrality of useful things is suggested by the various uses to which the same things are or can be put. The good scalpel can become a good weapon in the hands of an enraged medical assistant. Clearly many things that are regarded as good in the sense of useful come in time to be regarded as not good. It may be thought, accordingly, that the designation of something as *useful* is merely a 'way of speaking' about what is of interest to someone for some purpose and for some period of time. The idea of 'interest' as introduced here may be extended, of course, to things regarded as intrinsically good so as to suggest that all things of 'value' are in themselves ethically neutral. There comes to mind, in this connection, the following passage from Spinoza's *Ethics:*

> With regard to good and evil, these terms indicate nothing positive in things considered in themselves, nor are they anything else than modes of thought, or notions which we form from the comparison of one thing with another. For one and the same thing may at the same time be both good and evil or indifferent. Music, for example, is good to a melancholy person, bad to one mourning, while to a deaf man it is neither good nor bad.[14]

It should be said, first, that it is doubtful that any moral term is used, even by analogy, in a nonmoral sense or in place of a nonmoral term. If an individual speaks, for example, of a good knife, can it really be said that this expression is replaceable by

14. Baruch de Spinoza, *Ethics,* pt. 4, preface, trans. W. H. White in *Spinoza Selections,* ed. John Wild (New York: Charles Scribner's Sons, 1930), p. 285.

"sharp knife" or "stainless steel knife" or "durable knife" in the way that "sharp," "stainless steel," and "durable" are understood by the cutler or metallurgist? It is doubtful that a person who speaks of a good knife regularly considers its sharpness or stainlessness or durability apart from the operations in which the knife is involved or the ends to which the knife is applied. And this is precisely the point in the recognition of what is good in the sense of useful. 'Useful' signifies "being effective for . . ." and the goodness of a good knife involves its effectiveness (by virtue of its sharpness or whatever other property or properties) as a means to an end.[15]

In understanding that the term 'useful' always indicates a relation of means to an end, one recognizes the priority of final causes or ends over intrinsic causes or properties ('good-making' properties), which involve merely "hypothetical necessity."[16] If it is the relation of the scalpel to the purposes of the surgeon that indicates the scalpel's usefulness, then it is the use of the scalpel that indicates in turn the necessary properties of a good scalpel and not certain properties (sharpness, stainlessness, durability) that indicate use or effective use. In other words, the appraisal of things as useful involves directly the uses in which these things are effective and only indirectly the properties that these things possess. To think of a knife is to think of a kind of thing, either contrived to be used in one or many ways or adapted to be so used. A knife is thus distinct

15. A word must be said about the distinction between a 'knife' and a 'good knife'. There is a sense in which it is redundant to speak of a 'good knife'. It would be said that a knife in its definition is an instrument and therefore something which is *good* in the sense of useful. In recognition of this, and in order to avoid redundancy, one must mean by 'good knife' what is superior to other knives in utility or usefulness or what is the "best of its kind." When one speaks, accordingly, of a 'bad knife' one must mean what is ineffective in a certain operation or in relation to a certain purpose while being at the same time a thing which is *intended* to be used in this operation or for this purpose. One finds in a 'bad knife' a privation of effectiveness, either through fault in production or deterioration in use.

16. Cf. Aristotle, *Parts of Animals,* 1. 1, trans. A. L. Peck (Cambridge, Mass.: Harvard University Press, 1961), pp. 57-59.

from a stone, whose definition does not involve any relation to an extrinsic end (although, of course, one can speak of a keystone or cornerstone, whose definition does involve a relation to an extrinsic end). Every useful thing has its precise goodness as usefulness in virtue of its relation to some extrinsic end or purpose and not in virtue simply of its intrinsic properties. An end or purpose ("that for the sake of which"), whether as something good for its own sake or something good as a means to a further end, always enters into the determination of the precise usefulness of a particular thing.

There remains, however, the problem of the use of the terms 'good' and 'bad' by different individuals with respect to the same thing or by one individual with respect to the same thing under different circumstances. Such uses may seem to support the contention that moral terms represent subjective appraisals imposed upon a nonmoral realm. It is true, of course, that the same thing can be regarded as useful in different ways and that the thing believed to be good or useful in one situation may be viewed as useless in another situation. There is clearly a relativity in the usefulness of things, but this does not involve any difficulty for the intentionality and objectivity of moral judgments. There is no conflict or contradiction in offering different judgments concerning things as they stand in different relationships. A thing is useful or useless as determined with respect to a precise end and quite apart from a relation to any other end. Each judgment concerning what is useful is a matter of effectiveness of means to an end and is, accordingly, a judgment that is either correct or mistaken.

Intrinsic Good: The Good Man

The distinction between instrumental good and intrinsic good is carried in the distinction between the attributive, or adjunctive, use and the predicative use of the word 'good' (that is, "good in a certain respect" and "good simply or absolutely"). This distinction does not involve degrees of goodness. Clearly, anything that is good as a means can be taken as an end in itself, while most things that are good as ends are also good as means. A fine clock is recognizable as both useful in telling the hours of the day and as something to be prized as the "best of its kind." It is in the recognition of the intrinsic value of things, often useful things, that moral experience is most akin to aesthetic experience. A beautiful thing can be thought of simply as pleasing to see or to hear or to smell, where there is no involvement of desire and there is no impulse to possess the thing. A useful thing in its very completeness or perfection may also be pleasing and fascinating, although there would be an involvement of desire and there would be an impulse to acquire or to hold the thing as something both useful and worth having for its own sake. The completeness of the fine clock is the completeness of a useful thing as the "best of its kind." It is the consideration of the usefulness of the thing that brings about the appreciation of the thing for its own sake. It is the fine clock in its completeness *as a clock* that comes to be desired for itself. It is often the case that one recognizes the goodness of a fine timepiece without direct concern about the use of the timepiece to tell the hours of the day, as one recognizes the goodness of a fine violin or flute without any direct concern to use the instrument to play a tune.

There are, of course, intrinsic goods that are not completions or perfections of *making* but completions or perfections of activity or *doing.* One thinks, for example, of health as an intrinsic good which is final: it is a good which does not project beyond itself to any ulterior object. Health, of course, is 'useful' to the individual in relation to the numerous activities of daily life, but in itself or in its idea health does not embrace an extrinsic end. Health, like pleasure and moral virtue, can be thought about and cherished apart from any operation to be furthered or any purpose to be served.

Insofar as involvement with good things is an involvement with ends and with means, one may ask whether there is an end that is final and complete, an end that is neither a means to any good beyond itself nor merely a part of some composite good. It may be doubted at the outset that there is any object that can be both the beginning of desire or interest and its termination. And one may hold that all ends, with their appropriate means, are simply stages or steps to further ends in an open series of transient satisfactions. Thomas Hobbes has spoken of the succession of ends and of the transiency of satisfaction:

> . . . the felicity of this life, consisteth not in the repose of a mind satisfied. For there is no such *finus ultimus,* utmost aim, nor *summum bonum,* greatest good, as is spoken of in the books of the old moral philosophers. . . . Felicity is a continual progress of the desire, from one object to another; . . .[17]

The "old moral philosophers" whom Hobbes had in mind doubtless included Aristotle, who contended that if there were no final and complete good (τὸ ἄριστον) desiring would involve an infinite regress and would indeed be "futile and vain." It must be granted, of course, that desiring is always a desiring of something and that what is desired is in some way a terminus of appetite. The question is whether there is anything that can be *the* terminus of desire and that is, accordingly, the genuine and ultimate object of all interests of whatever sort.

An approach in answer to this question can be made through the consideration of the things that are desired for themselves and not simply for their usefulness. If indeed the individual is able to involve himself in the experience of a series of objects whose satisfactions are replaceable by what is ever new and fascinating, then one must accept Hobbes' notion of the continual movement of desire. This would require, of course, the abandonment of the idea of intrinsic value, for if a thing and the satisfaction that follows from its possession are replaceable and surpassable, nothing can be sought for its own sake. But it appears in our moral experience that there are things, such as health and friendship, that are pursued for their own sake and whose gratifications are not replaceable as the satisfaction of eating one chestnut is replaceable by the satisfaction of eating another chestnut. To recognize things of intrinsic value is to

17. Hobbes, *Leviathan,* chap. 11, p. 63. Cf. Thomas Hobbes, *Human Nature; or the Fundamental Elements of Policy,* in *The English Works of Thomas Hobbes,* ed. Sir William Molesworth (London: John Bohn, 1839-45), 4:33.

recognize that desire does not move continually from one object to another but has as many termini as there are things whose possession is irreplaceable and whose gratification is unsurpassable.

There remains, however, the question whether beyond the several termini of desire in things that are intrinsically good there is one terminus of all desire, namely, a final and complete good, as Aristotle would hold and Hobbes would deny. The clue to the answer to this question can be found in the enumeration of intrinsic goods. In recognizing that any list of precise goods would likely be incomplete, one can talk of categories of intrinsic goods, namely, aesthetic objects and enjoyments, intellectual excellence, the moral virtues, association and friendship, and health. It is apparent that such kinds of things are good *for* the individual. This is not simply to say that an individual considers his own *being* as embracing in its completeness such intrinsic goods as constituents. The completeness of the individual is rather the full activity of life involving a range of completions or perfections. For all individuals this activity of life is, contrary to Hobbes, the *utmost aim* and *greatest good.*

To speak of human good as the completeness of individual life is to have in mind an end that is compatible, although not interchangeable, with *being.* We have commented earlier upon one seemingly insoluble problem of modern ethical discussion, namely, the relevance of moral norms to what empirical evidence reveals to be the "real" order of things and to what the actual behavior of individuals suggests to be the direct and "significant" concerns of human life. One may well contend in this connection that moral discussion does not and cannot lead to the discovery of any "ultimate aim" that can be taken to have status as the real or actual. In contrast to the realm of fact, one would argue, there is the "realm" of value by the "recognition" of which one's affairs can be "ordered" but of which one cannot in the very nature of the case have knowledge or certainty.

What is not made clear in any separation of value from fact is just how an individual can conduct his affairs and sustain his purposes according to 'norms' of human life that are not real as human life itself is real. The separation of value from fact with respect to what is *real* becomes the cleavage between *aiming* and *knowing*, in which presumably aiming must go on without the benefit of knowing. From this it would follow that moral dispositions of one sort or another must somehow generate their own "objects" in the pursuit of what one customarily thinks of as the well-being of the individual. But one cannot, of course, really speak of *well-being* if there is no state or condition of human life that can be known and accepted as "living well." The very idea of *well-being* (as a state of *being*) loses significance. One escapes or avoids all of this simply in holding that there is an *object* of interest and striving which is the discovery of thought. Thus it can be said that there is a rational attachment to what *as a whole* an individual is able to become, or to any part thereof to which an individual aspires or strives, as an ignorant man would perfect his mind or a sick man would regain his health.

The attention to the dispositional as opposed to the cognitive, in seeking an alternative approach to the meaning of 'goodness', involves the consideration of attitudes apart from aspiration as the rational pursuit of the good. In shifting the foundation of the moral life from the *recognitions* of moral awareness to the *dispositions* of moral experience, it follows that ethical discussion cannot be a clarification and refinement of moral judgment and that there is no *reasonable* path for the moral life to take. David Hume has given a classic statement of this shift in the foundation of morals:

> The impressions, which arise from good and evil most naturally, and with the least preparation are the *direct* passions of desire and aversion, grief and joy, hope and fear, along with volition. The mind by an *original* instinct tends to unite itself with the good, and to avoid the evil. . . . Our decisions concerning moral rectitude and depravity are evidently perceptions; . . . Morality, therefore, is more properly felt than judg'd of. . . .[18]

18. Hume, *A Treatise of Human Nature*, bk 2., pt. 3, sec. 9; bk. 3, pt. 1, sec. 2, pp. 438, 470.

It is not clear just what this passage seeks to establish. To say that goodness or rightness is presented through a disposition such as feeling or emotion can be taken to mean either that feeling or emotion is the good or that feeling or emotion is a way of knowing what is good. If the intention is to maintain that it is through feeling that good is encountered or experienced by the individual, then feeling is put forward as a faculty that is cognitive of moral values, as other things are encountered or experienced through other ways of knowing. But the argument here is devious. For at first there is an appeal *against* cognition *to* consciousness as feeling or emotion and then there is the recognition of feeling or emotion as being itself cognitive or perceptive. Apart from the apparent contradiction, it is difficult to see how *feeling* is also *knowing*. It would seem that feeling is simply feeling, and that in restricting one's concerns in moral matters to feelings one embraces noncognitivism. If one wants somehow to think of affective experience as perceptive and discriminating, one must allow that feeling in this respect is indistinguishable from intuition and that what is grasped in affective experience is indistinguishable, as truth, from what is gained through rational insight and judgment. But to allow this is to abandon noncognitivism.[19]

19. It is not amiss to place David Hume among the romanticists of the eighteenth century, along with Vico and Herder, who rejected or appeared to reject reason in order to recognize and endorse feeling as an apprehensive faculty which moves the will or heart. The complex character of Hume's stand on feeling and reason is apparent, however, from the following passage in his *Enquiry Concerning the Principles of Morals,* ed. L. A. Selby-Bigge, rev. P. H. Nidditch (Oxford: The Clarendon Press, 1975), sec. 1, pp. 172-73: "The end of all moral speculations is to teach us our duty; . . . But is this ever to be expected from inferences and conclusions of the understanding, which of themselves have no hold of the affections nor set in motion the active powers of men . . . What is honorable, what is fair, what is becoming, what is noble, what is generous, takes possession of the heart, and animates us to embrace and maintain it. . . . I am apt to suspect . . . that *reason* and *sentiment* concur in almost all moral determinations and conclusions. The final sentence, it is probable, which pronounces characters and actions amiable or odious . . . depends on some internal sense or feeling, which nature has made universal in the whole species. . . . But in order to pave the way for such a sentiment, and

The appeal to feeling rejects rational intersubjectivity in moral matters only to come to intersubjectivity in a different way. In the appeal to feeling, there is apparently a "way of knowing" in morals that precludes error through the immediacy or directness of what Hume calls "original instinct." At the same time, there is no barrier to moral agreement among those who have the same or similar perceptions. But there is, in this shift to feeling, the loss of discourse about the moral life through the use of moral language in judgment and argument. The exclusion of moral concerns from the realm of reason and discourse appears to be urged upon us without justification and without any gain in the understanding of the place of feeling and reason in human experience. The appreciation of feeling's part in the moral life does not require the substitution of feeling or "original instinct" for rational apprehension. Feeling attends the whole range of human awareness, and moral experience in being affective does not for that reason lack a foundation in what reason is able to grasp of the nature of things.

If the advocate of the primacy of feeling in moral experience does not wish to maintain that feeling or emotion is cognitive but only to hold that feeling or emotion is the good, one is constrained to reject this also. One can certainly grant, as Socrates is represented as affirming in the *Protagoras,* that feeling as pleasure is good—pleasure is indeed that feeling of which one rightly predicates the term 'good'. But one is not called upon to grant, as Hume seems to require, that feeling or pleasure (i.e., whatever is immediately or ultimately pleasant to one individual or to others) is what goodness is. For to say this is simply to reduce all attainment and satisfaction to the affective life of the individual and to ignore all of the other ways in which an individual can be fulfilled and all of the other kinds of things that pertain to the completeness of the individual. F. H. Bradley has made this point in the following way:

---

give a proper discernment of its object, it is often necessary, we find, that much reasoning should precede, that nice distinctions be made, just conclusions be drawn, distant comparisons formed, complicated relations examined, and general facts fixed and ascertained."

> We are . . . mistaken when we attempt to set up any one aspect of our nature as supreme, and to regard the other aspects merely as conducive and subject to its rule. . . . mere pleasure is an abstraction which we make from what is pleasant. . . . We are forced in reason to distinguish between pleasure and that which is pleasant, and so far as I see, we cannot in reason make the second of these subject to the first. We may put it otherwise by saying that, where pleasure exists, it is the whole man who feels the pleasure, the whole man with all of his practical and other activities and the complete range of his emotions.[20]

The goodness of "the whole man," to use Bradley's phrase, is both comprehensive and final. The constituents of this goodness are intrinsic goods, each of which contributes to the character of the individual to whom a term such as 'happy' or 'virtuous' is applicable. It would seem that all moral and legal matters, as concerns about human affairs, derive their direction and force from the recognition of individual human existence viewed both in itself and as the end of all social and legal means. This primacy of the individual was set forth initially in the testimony of Socrates, in the *Apology,* in which he sought to arouse his fellow citizens to a concern about themselves, a concern about their individual lives as excellent or mean and about their actions as noble or base.

The Final Good and the Rights of Persons

A matter which remains is that of stating with some clarity and precision just what the norm of "the good man" means as an aid in the ordering of human affairs. This is the problem of distinguishing the constituents of individual well-being, particularly since the support of these things is thought to be the concern of all or most members of a society. We have mentioned earlier the categories of goods that can be taken to be desirable or worth having for their own sake. One must continue to inquire, however, concerning what all or most individ-

20. F. H. Bradley, *Essays on Truth and Reality* (Oxford: The Clarendon Press, 1914), pp. 3, 5.

uals would be expected to want for themselves and to secure for themselves, inasmuch as there is no ready agreement among the members of society as to what are the good things they should have. The search for an answer to this question might lead an investigator to consult his own aspirations and satisfactions and to interrogate others, in Socratic fashion, about their aspirations and satisfactions. A good deal of attention has in fact been given to this matter by anthropologists and sociologists who have been concerned with the prevailing values of a society and with conflicts of values both within and between cultures. The difficulty with this approach, of course, is the possibility of confusion between what is prescribed in a society and what is indeed desirable or estimable. This confusion is able to occur simply because the prevailing norms of a society or group determine in that society or group what is expected of its members, although such norms may not in fact represent what the members or at least some of the members expect (as estimable) for themselves. Whether any prevailing norm represents for an individual what is estimable is a matter that can be determined directly by consulting the individual concerning what in his judgment are the things that are most valuable. Such a consultation shifts the matter from social science to ethics, from the character of society to the character and capability of the individual, and thus avoids an egregious confusion between social reality and moral possibility.

This shift, which is at bottom a shift from the character of society to the character of man, does not really settle the matter at hand. Philosophical anthropology would seem to offer as diverse an array of views about human nature as cultural anthropology or sociology offers about prevailing moral practice. In the attention, however, to what Aristotle calls "states of life" or consciousness (*τά ἐν νῇ ψυχῇ γινόμενα*), one is able to distinguish basic tendencies and capacities (*δυνάμεις*) in the total aspiring or aiming of the individual and to consider the individual as behaving under his own guidance and not simply in response to the promptings of impulse or feeling. We come then to think of human tendencies and capacities as underlying what we recognize as intrinsic or final goods and as supporting what we recognize as the rights of the individual or person.

Few accounts of human nature and human interest have matched the straightforwardness of Hobbes' analysis of the man in the *Leviathan.* In his long and detailed discussion, Hobbes gives attention primarily to the one motive of self-interest, that is, to the interest in the use of power to preserve oneself. The difficulty in Hobbes' account is the abstraction of egoistic disposition from the tendencies and capacities that are to be advanced or fulfilled through self-preservation. One is constrained to say, against Hobbes, that a creature of rational intelligence, in seeking to preserve himself, would be guided at the same time by other demands of his conscious life. Hobbes would seem to recognize this in commenting that where there is a preoccupation with the devices of physical survival and security there is precluded the cultivation of the productive, noëtic, and social arts.[21] When he speaks of organized society, Hobbes is careful to point out that it is the duty of the sovereign power to support the full safety of the people, embracing all "contentments of life." But Hobbes does not speak of the 'rights' of the individual with respect to the constituents of a life of contentment, except in reference to those *liberties* that "depend on the silence of the law." His attention to the constant threat of one's enemies brings him to talk chiefly of the 'right of nature' (*ius naturae*) as the liberty of "doing any thing" to protect one's life and members. Accordingly, for Hobbes, political society itself rests upon the common need for restriction of this absolute right of nature rather than upon the recognition of natural rights as moral claims upon the constituents of a complete life. The basic confusion in Hobbes' thought concerning the nature of man and the nature of organized society is obscured by the sustained attention he gives to the individual's interest in survival and security in abstraction from the context of human tendencies and interests as a whole.

St. Thomas Aquinas, writing centuries before Hobbes, recognized the whole of human tendency and interest in saying that "reason of its nature apprehends the things toward which man

21. Hobbes, *Leviathan,* chap. 13, p. 82.

has a natural tendency as good objectives, and therefore to be actively pursued, . . . and their contraries as bad, and therefore to be shunned."[22] If there is a *right* to preserve one's life, there are other *rights* to other objects of demand. In his concern about himself, the individual is able to identify *claims* upon genuine goods as distinct from interests in and pretensions to merely apparent goods. The claims upon genuine goods are seen, at the same time, to indicate what actions are appropriate in obtaining and preserving these very things. To the considera-tion of the nature of appropriate or right conduct we now turn.

22. St. Thomas Aquinas, *Summa Theologiae,* First Part of the Second Part, Q. 94, A. 1, trans. Thomas Gilby, O. P. (London: Eyre and Spottis-woode, Ltd., 1966).

3 *The Right*

Actions and Consequences

It is more difficult, perhaps, to talk of right action or rightness than it is to talk of goodness. While what a man does is indeed a part of what he is as a good man and what he affirms as a good citizen, there is the problem of the determination of what an individual is to do in particular and complex situations involving his interests and the interests of others. Inasmuch as actions have consequences and are in this sense productive of good or bad ends, one may well hold that ends *as consequences* (or probable consequences) must enter into any and all considerations of actions as right or wrong. At the same time, there is often in our experience the opposition or antinomy between what is 'right' as a means to some end and what is 'right' as *fitting,* that is, as appropriate to the demands or expectations of rational beings or persons considered as ends in themselves. One recognizes with Kant that there can be no deliberate action without the thought of some end.[1] The fundamental question, then, concerns the character of the end or ends of deliberate action. This question has a long history and has been the center

1. Cf. Immanuel Kant, *Metaphysics of Morals: The Doctrine of Virtue,* trans. Mary J. Gregor (New York: Harper and Row, Publishers, 1964), pp. 38-39.

of a long debate between teleologists and deontologists, between those who take the view that 'right' is what is productive of or conducive to the good and those who hold that 'right' is what is directly apprehended as self-justifying action quite apart from the proximate consequences that flow therefrom.

One may be moved to ask, in this connection, whether the opposition between teleologists and deontologists is perchance more apparent than real. And it may be pointed out that teleologists (for example, utilitarians) who are concerned about the promotion of general happiness would seem to hold a view of right action that is, in some aspects at least, deontological. If the individual is to promote the well-being of others, it may be argued, there must be a criterion of right action other than the maintenance of a balance of pleasure over pain, namely, the criterion of consistency of action (as duty) with the purposes of other persons. Without such a guide in behavior, it would be merely problematic that an individual would act in a way beneficial to "the greatest number" of human beings. In other words, the appeal to felicitous consequences alone as the ends by which actions are judged to be 'right' would seem to leave undetermined the precise beneficiaries of such actions. An individual could conceivably act to maximize the happiness of selected individuals and deliberately ignore the happiness of others without being involved in any action that would be regarded as wrong.[2]

Even with respect to the individual's support of his own

2. Cf. Henry Sidgwick, *The Methods of Ethics*, 7th ed. (Chicago: The University of Chicago Press, 1962), pp. 416-17: "In all cases . . . it becomes practically important to ask whether any mode of distributing a given quantum of happiness is better than any other. Now the Utilitarian formula seems to supply no answer to this question: at least we have to supplement the principle of seeking the greatest happiness on the whole by some principle of Just and Right distribution of this happiness. The principle which most Utilitarians have either tacitly or expressly adopted is that of pure equality—as given in Bentham's formula, 'everybody to count for one, and nobody for more than one'. And this principle seems to be the only one which does not need a special justification; for, as we saw, it must be reasonable to treat any one man in the same way as any other, if there be no reason apparent for treating him differently."

concerns, the appeal to felicitous consequences does not appear to cover the whole range of what the individual would recognize as right action. The attention to consequences again finds itself opposed by considerations about what is "fitting" or "becoming" for the agent, quite apart from the presumed consequences of his action. Action productive or thought to be productive of favorable consequences is often regarded as inappropriate. An individual finds himself reluctant to eavesdrop upon another individual's conversation, although such eavesdropping would likely provide information advantageous to himself and to his friends. And this reluctance may express itself in such a declaration as "I find eavesdropping repugnant" or "One simply does not eavesdrop." If 'right action' is always what is productive or what is believed to be productive of some end or ends, there would simply be no possibility of an experience of reluctance to do what clearly pertains in a positive way to such end or ends. One may say, of course, that this "reluctance" is merely *affective* and reflects nothing more than the peculiarity of an individual's sensibility or upbringing. But this would not really dispose of the disinclination to eavesdrop as morally exceptional or spurious. One could as well regard the inclination to advance one's interests as morally spurious and the disinclination to eavesdrop as morally genuine. Moral questions can hardly be settled by appeals to or against sensibilities of one sort or another. The preference for any action as "fitting" really involves the action itself as viewed in a setting of individuals who make demands upon one another in the exercise of their rights as persons.

Actions and Intentions

Rightness is a matter of intention. Intention (*intentio*) in *thought* is a directing of the mind toward some thing as an object.[3] Intention in *action* is an expression or thrust of the

3. Cf. St. Augustine, *De Trinitate,* 11. 2. 2, trans. Arthur W. Haddan (Edinburgh: T. and T. Clark, 1873), p. 263: ". . . that attention of the mind which keeps the sense in that which we see, and connects both . . . : this attention is the act of the mind alone. . . ."

will toward an object taken as an end.[4] Many intentions as actions are simply affirmations or pledges. The intention in extending one's hand in greeting another individual is to affirm or support the status of the individual as a friend or guest. The intention in uttering or repeating a vow is to affirm or reaffirm a commitment or union of one sort or another. But intention in action is often both an *affirmation* through overt behavior and a *projection* of consequences deriving from overt behavior. All actions have ends as referents but not all ends or referents are consequences. Assisting a child in the learning of a language would be in intention *right,* both as an affirmation of the child's rational capability to learn a language and as a furthering of the child's intellectual development as a concomitant or consequence of language instruction. At the same time, telling a seriously ill person the facts about his physical condition would be *right* as an affirmation of his rationality and the corresponding claim upon the truth, even though the precise consequences of such truth telling are unpredictable. Intention is the formal rightness of action, as distinguishable from what in fact obtains as the consequence or consequences of action. The eighteenth-century moralist Richard Price has put the matter in these words:

> It is the actual conformity of the wills of moral agents to what they see or believe to be the fitnesses of things, that is the object of our praise or esteem. One of these may, perhaps, very properly be called the virtue of the action, in contradistinction from the other, which may be called the virtue of the agent. To the former, no particular intention is requisite . . . to the other the particular intention is what is most essential. . . . Our own determinations alone are, most properly, our actions. . . . There seems indeed scarcely any thing more evident, than that there are two views or senses, in which we commonly speak of actions. Sometimes we mean by them, the determinations or voli-

4. Cf. *De Trinitate,* 8. 6. 9: ". . . that mind is righteous which knowingly and of purpose assigns to everyone his due in life and behavior. . . ."

> tions themselves of a being, of which the intention is an essential part: And sometimes we mean the real event, or external effect produced.[5]

Intention as 'formal rightness' is the consistency of action with the status or worth of individuals as persons and, accordingly, with what is believed to be beneficial rather than harmful to the individual. All deliberate action in society has as a direct referent some individual whose status as a person requires such action toward him as will affirm his worth and will support, in accordance with this worth, his life activity as a whole. The intention of right action embraces consequences without being determined simply by consequences. One can never set out, as Kant observed, from the consideration of consequences or probable consequences alone in order to determine what is the right thing to do, for example, to tell the truth in a particular matter. Whether or not I speak the truth at a given moment is problematic where the determination of action rests entirely upon my immediate interest in desirable consequences of one sort or another. It is only when the individual to whom I speak is brought into the moral frame of reference that lying can be seen as morally wrong, whatever the desirable consequences that are believed to follow from this or that instance of lying. For it is only then that I can see that every possible favorable consequence of lying to this individual is to be gained in disregard of the claim of a rational being upon the truth and in manipulation of the individual as a *thing.* The intention of a right act is thus an affirmation of human worth or dignity, which necessarily excludes certain consequences whose production would involve an offense or offenses against worth or dignity. One must set out from such a basic affirmation in order to ascertain just what consequences are compatible with personal existence and with relationships among persons. Without a reference to persons, *action* or doing becomes indistinguishable from *production* or making, as in all moral and political

5. Richard Price, *A Review of the Principal Questions in Morals,* in *British Moralists,* ed. L. A. Selby-Bigge (Indianapolis: The Bobbs-Merrill Company, Inc., 1964), 2:179.

theories that view right action as a means merely to some end.

The important distinction between behavior productive of desirable consequences and right or fitting conduct has been made by Joseph Butler. In *The Analogy of Religion,* Bishop Butler writes as follows:

> . . . we must distinguish between *actions* themselves and that *quality* ascribed to them, which we call virtuous or vicious. The gratification itself of every natural passion, must be attended with delight; and acquisitions of fortune, however made, are acquisitions of the means or materials of enjoyment. . . . To say that such an action or course of behavior, procured such pleasure or advantage, or brought such inconvenience and pain, is quite a different thing from saying, that such good or bad effect was owing to the virtue or vice of such action or behavior. In one case, an action abstracted from all moral consideration, produced its effect; in the other case . . . the morality or viciousness of it, produced the effect.[6]

The distinction between what is merely productive of desirable consequences and what is right is simply the distinction between the efficacy of effort toward any end whatsoever and the appropriateness of action to the worth of persons in a community. Appropriateness or fitness of action clearly embraces consequences such as the gaining of "pleasure or advantage" and the avoidance of "inconvenience and pain" but only as consequences that fall within the scope of respect for persons and justice among persons. The intention of right action has as its referent the totality of persons considered with respect to both individual and common good. In the intention of right action, each individual is an object of ultimate concern. In affirming and supporting the full range of possibilities open to

6. Joseph Butler, *The Analogy of Religion to the Constitution and Course of Nature* (Philadelphia: J. B. Lippincott and Company, 1871), pp. 111-12. Cf. Butler, *Dissertation II: Of the Nature of Virtue,* in *British Moralists,* 1:246: "For as much as it has been disputed wherein virtue consists . . . there is in reality an universally acknowledged standard of it . . . namely, justice, veracity, and regard to common good."

the individual as a person and as a member of a community of equals, moral or right action is humane and provident.

What is critical here is the acceptance of individuals as members of the moral community. The rightness of truth telling, for example, is blurred or overturned by the failure or inability to recognize an individual as other than an aid or hindrance to one's purposes or the purposes of one's party or group. If the end of human existence and human association is the direct realization of individual interests and demands, of whatever sorts, then it is nonsense to talk of right conduct as that which affirms and supports the worth or dignity of persons. All deliberate behavior presupposes some idea or image of the status or "position" of other individuals. If individuals are not ends in themselves, then truth telling, keeping promises, benevolence, and the like cannot be projected as actions to be carried out as alternatives to the direct pursuit of self-interest. In the recognition of individuals as members of a single moral community, on the other hand, all of the rational sanctions of mutual esteem are invoked and all of the justifications of rugged self-interest are obviated.

The community of persons is in its very idea an open, unlimited association. In any effort to limit the scope of the community, the individual encounters conflicts between what is right in relations with individuals who are within the limited community and what is right in relations with individuals who are outside it. If any individual is to be regarded as an outsider, then one must in some way deny to this individual the status (as a person) that is enjoyed by an insider.[7] One faces a moral

7. Cf. Henri Bergson, *The Two Sources of Morality and Religion* (New York: Henry Holt and Co., 1935). Concerning the Greek notion of justice, Bergson says: "The progress which was decisive for the substance of justice . . . consisted in the substitution of a universal republic, embracing all men, for that republic which went no farther than the gates of the city, and within the city, was limited to free men. . . . There is nothing more instructive than to see how the philosophers have skirted round it, touched it, and yet missed it. Let us leave out Plato, who certainly includes the Idea of man among the transcendent Ideas: did it not follow that all men were of the same essence? From this to the idea that all men,

predicament in which the same act is both virtuous and vicious; in which what is owed to one individual in relation to his needs is not owed to another individual having the same needs; in which, in short, *rightness* varies in accordance with the social predilections and commitments of the agent.

The idea of one community of persons transcends but does not overturn the limited community existing as village, city, or state. All limited communities are parts of the one community, as all members of limited communities are members of the one community.[8] The norm of all limited communities, with respect to the status of the individual, is the norm of the community of all persons. Each limited community, insofar as it does not ignore the well-being of the individual, supports the *idea of community* through the organization of functions and the distribution of goods and services for the sake of those who find themselves or place themselves under the care of the community. The effective work of the limited community would be determined by the adequacy of resources with respect to the needs of individuals, thus distinguishing the organized life of cities and states from the organized life of villages and towns.

---

qua men, were of equal worth and that the common essence conferred on them the same fundamental rights, was but one step. But the step was not taken. It would have meant condemning slavery, giving up the Greek idea that foreigners, being barbarians, could claim no rights" (p. 68).

8. Cf. Josiah Royce, *The Hope of the Great Community*, in *The Basic Writings of Josiah Royce*, ed. John J. McDermott (Chicago: The University of Chicago Press, 1969), 2:1150-52: ". . . the sign of an ideal community of all the faithful . . . is a bare suggestion of that ideal of the community of mankind which it was the historic mission of Christianity to introduce into the world . . . and to hold before the world for the healing of the nations. The present situation of humanity depends upon the fact that for good reasons, which have to do not merely with the sentimental and romantic aspirations of humanity, but also with the most serious business in which men are engaged, the idea of community has become more concrete, more closely related to the affairs of daily life, has become more practicable than ever before. . . . The belief that mankind can be and in the end shall be one, has thus for a long time had an increased concreteness, definiteness, practical applicability, and despite all the vast evils of our modern social order, a genuine hopefulness."

Right Actions and the Rights of Persons

To speak of individuals as persons and as equals is to introduce into the discussion of rightness the notion of *rights*. What is meant by 'person' is simply the rational consciousness in its openness to truth and to the responsibilities of rational self-determination in a community. If there are persons, there are claims upon the truth and upon opportunities for self-fulfillment. The agent as a person would act properly or rightly in accordance with his own claims and in support of the claims of others. Claims, viewed as anterior to social and political conventions and permissions, are *rights*, and rights are the properties of equals. Equality of rights does not mean that all persons are expected to exercise claims upon the same precise things; rather, it is compatible with diversity in interest and need. What is wrong or blameworthy in the exercise of rights in a community is unilateral action of individuals for their own exclusive advantage. There can be no right *in a community* to act in contempt of the claims of others. The right to preserve one's life can have no moral justification when expressed, as it is by Hobbes, as "a right to every thing; even to one another's body."[9] The same limitation of exercise would apply to other rights, such as the right to property.[10] Even what is recognized as the right to develop one's talents can have moral justification only where there is the affirmation by one individual of equal opportunity for the development of the talents of others. Some of the difficulties in determining the extent of exercise of rights in society are avoided in recognizing that rights are *in idea* things of limit.

This point is apparent if one thinks of rights and right actions in relation to freedom. Human freedom is self-determination

9. Hobbes, *Leviathan,* chap. 14.

10. Cf. John Locke, *The Second Treatise of Civil Government,* ed. J. W. Gough (Oxford: Basil Blackwell, 1948), chap. 5, p. 19: "I dare boldly affirm—that the same rule of propriety, viz., that every man should have as much as he could make use of, would hold still in the world without straitening anybody . . . had not the invention of money, and the tacit agreement of men to put a value on it, introduced (by consent) larger possessions and a right to them. . . ."

within a community. The freedom to act as one pleases, in accordance with a presumed "right to every thing" and in indifference to the interests and needs of others, would be the freedom of the solitary individual or the freedom of the strong or clever person. This freedom would be defective either in lacking the benefits of association and cooperation or in enjoying those benefits in a parasitic way. Richard Hooker in the sixteenth century spoke of freedom as rational coexistence:

> . . . forasmuch as we are not ourselves sufficient to furnish ourselves with competent store of things, needful for such a life as our nature doth desire, a life fit for the dignity of man; therefore to supply those defects and imperfections which are in us, as living simply and solely by ourselves, we are naturally inclined to seek communion and fellowship with others. This was the cause of men's uniting themselves at the first in politic Societies, which societies could not be without Government, nor Government without a distinct kind of Law . . . .[11]

This must not be taken to mean that right action is what is determined by social or political agreement. Ethical concerns cannot be annulled by what are held to be extra-ethical demands arising from social or political expedience. Right action is the action that both affirms and accords with the rights of persons constituting a community of equals. Right action, in other words, is what would be agreed upon by those who accept the norm of respect for persons as the basis of social order and social justice.[12] This is the conduct of individuals who recognize the opportunities and the constraints of freedom and who seek to establish and maintain an order of justice under

11. Richard Hooker, *Of the Laws of Ecclesiastical Polity* (London: J. M. Dent and Sons, Ltd., 1954), 1:188. Cf., J.-J. Rousseau, *The Social Contract,* 1. 8, and Aristotle, *Politics,* 1. 1. 9-12.

12. Cf. John Rawls, *A Theory of Justice* (Cambridge, Mass.: Harvard University Press, 1971), p. 17: "It is clear . . . that . . . one conception of justice is more reasonable than another, or justifiable with respect to it, if rational persons in the initial situation would choose its principles over those of the other for the role of justice. Conceptions of justice are to be ranked by their acceptability to persons so circumstanced."

which each individual is responsible for the freedom of the community as a whole. Right action, freedom, and justice are interchangeable notions.

One faces, however, the difficult problem of distinguishing classes or categories of actions through which the advantage of all persons in a community would be promoted without conflict and injury. Categories of right actions correspond with the categories of needs. At the risk of simplifying what is complex, one dares to mention broad categories of needs, namely, physical comfort and security, intellectual and aesthetic cultivation, and association. One thinks of efforts to satisfy these needs as the contributing parts of a consistent program of human good. With respect to the needs distinguishable within any category —for example, physical comfort and security—there would of course arise questions concerning the precise actions to be carried out for the sake of particular goods. The resolution of such questions would require agreement as to what is *essential* to human comfort and security and what is peripheral or indeed harmful, whatever the variations and distortions in human desires.[13]

In a completely coherent order of conduct, all actual and conceivable right actions would be carried out free of conflict and no performance of one action would prevent or hinder the performance of another. One does not imagine that such an order of conduct would be realizable except in a small, uniform community. One can imagine as workable in any community, however, a scheme of *sustaining actions* (truth telling, promise keeping, the obligations of distributive justice, the obligations of remedial justice, benevolence) through which the life and freedom of persons can be supported,[14] a scheme providing at

13. Cf. Aristotle, *Politics,* 1. 3. 9, trans. H. Rackham (Cambridge, Mass.: Harvard University Press, 1972): ". . . it is of these goods [which are necessary for life and useful for the community of city or household] that riches in the true sense at all events seem to consist. For the amount of such property sufficient in itself for a good life is not unlimited. . . . for a limit has been fixed, as with the other arts, since no tool belonging to any art is without a limit whether in number or in size, and riches are a collection of tools for the householder and the statesman."

14. Cf. Bernard Bosanquet, *The Philosophical Theory of the State*

the same time the moral structure of a body of civil law.[15] This order of sustaining actions would embrace *permissible actions,* which do not in idea conflict with sustaining actions and which pertain to the freedom of the individual in some matters to do or not to do.[16] There would remain a "surd" of conflicts within the order of sustaining actions—for examples, the conflict between truth telling and the keeping of confidence, between refraining from injuring another and injuring another in self-defense. Moral dilemmas of this sort, as distinct from resolvable or merely apparent moral conflicts, are irreducible *in principle.* They arise from the irreducible complexity of human life and from the moral divergence of associative and dissociative behavior.

One may be tempted to find a way out of such difficulties through the idea of the relativity of all action to circumstances or through the idea of the subordination of certain actions or duties to others as circumstances require. The inadequacy of any qualification of the rightness of action has been pointed

---

(London: Macmillan and Company, Ltd., 1965), p. 157: "*Prima facie,* there may be, as with systems which compose the mind, all degrees of alliance, indifference, or opposition between . . . groupings of persons; and the same person, belonging to many different groups, may find his diverse 'capacities' apparently at variance with one another. A conscientious Trade Unionist may find his capacity as a member of the Union, interpreted as binding him to do his utmost for the amelioration of working class conditions in general, apparently at variance with his capacity as the head of a family bound to provide immediately for those whom he has brought into the world. Or a judge or magistrate, obliged to enforce what he conceives to be a bad law, may find his official capacity apparently at variance with his duty as a conscientious citizen. It is plain that unless, on the whole, a working harmony were maintained between the different groups which form society, life could not go on."

15. Cf. John Henry Merryman, *The Civil Law Tradition* (Stanford: Stanford University Press, 1969), pp. 98-108.

16. Cf. Georg Henrik von Wright, *Norm and Action. A Logical Inquiry* (London: Routledge and Kegan Paul, Ltd., 1963), p. 144: ". . . a set of commands and permissions is consistent (the norms compatible) if, and only if, it is logically possible, under any given condition of application, to obey *all* the commands collectively and avail oneself of *each one* of the permissions individually which apply on that condition."

out by H. A. Prichard in what he says against the relativity of duty:

> . . . the term 'absolute' applied to 'duty' can only add emphasis. There cannot be two kinds of duty, the one absolute and the other not. Either we are bound to do something or we are not; we cannot be bound to do something but not absolutely.[17]

It would seem that the determination of what is right or fitting, as sustaining rather than permissible action, is ultimate: there can be no further consideration of what should be done or of the incentives for acting in a certain way. This means that right or fitting action carries with it the idea and force of what is binding or obligatory, thus arousing a distinct volitional response beyond the appeal of other incentives to act in other ways. The awareness of what is right or fitting is, then, the awareness of what is obligatory. This is to say that the individual, in knowing of what is right or fitting, knows of obligation. If one could know what is right or fitting without recognizing such action as the fitting object of the will, one could somehow know what should be done without indeed knowing what should be done. The obligation to act in a certain way rests simply upon the character of the action itself as present to the moral awareness of the individual. The individual cannot *know* what is right (and binding upon him) and have this knowledge overturned or rendered nugatory by considerations extrinsic to his knowing.

To recognize that all action occurs in a situation (that is, in a context or milieu that is formed in part by circumstances) is not to allow that the determination of rightness is relative to circumstances. Circumstances as such are morally blind and uninstructive, and no appeal to circumstances can settle a moral question. To find oneself unexpectedly without funds to purchase one's supper would not itself indicate what one should do, whether to steal food, rob a passerby, drop in upon a

17. H. A. Prichard, "Moral Obligation," in *Moral Obligation. Essays and Lectures* (Oxford: The Clarendon Press, 1949), p. 147.

neighbor or friend, or simply go without supper. What is done in this situation will be one out of a number of possible actions, all of which are in accord with the same circumstances. What is right or fitting in this situation will be indicated by the individual's appreciation of the rights of others as well as by the awareness of his own plight. One must say, then, that the recognition of the rights of persons and of the limits of these rights under the reciprocal freedom of a community is illuminative of what is fitting or reasonable behavior in particular situations. In every situation the individual must act so as to exploit the circumstances or conditions of human existence for the sake of distinctly human ends.

4 *Justice*

Morality and Law: The Historic Setting

There is a direct relationship between morality and law. Individuals as social beings live under regulations of one sort or another and in being concerned about themselves are directly concerned about the *fairness* of the rules by which they are governed. The fact that legal procedure has to do chiefly with the meaning and application of existing law and with legal precedents established in various ways does not affect at all the pertinence of moral discussion to legal matters. To any individual apprehended by the police or convicted by a jury or sentenced to jail by a judge, it is a primary concern whether or not at each stage of the legal process he has received his due as a citizen and as a person. Aristotle recognized that law is inseparable from morals and that considerations of justice belong to ethics, in his view that justice in the broadest sense is simply the whole of virtue practiced with respect to others, that is to say, practiced in a social context. The presumption of good order, then, is that the laws prescribe only what is reasonable and fitting and that the enactment of laws is merely part of the effort of an organized society to support the virtue or goodness of its members. A law that is not the best ordering of means to end is, accordingly, a defective or unjust law or simply no law at all.

To speak of the relation of governance to the well-being of the governed is to think of the rights and duties of the governed. A right is an indefeasible claim of an individual upon a status or condition of existence. Ultimately all rights, however distinguished and enumerated, arise from the pretension of a rational being to the freedom of an autonomous life. Insofar as this freedom is to be enjoyed in a social context, there must be a concern of rational beings to establish the best *order* for their mutual benefit. Both as formal recognition of claims upon positive goods and as formal guarantee of redress of injuries, every scheme of law and order would have its foundation in a bill or charter of rights rather than in a covenant or contract. All theories of the social contract express, directly or indirectly, either the position of Glaucon in Plato's *Republic*[1] or the position of John Locke in his *Second Treatise of Civil Government.*[2] Glaucon held that covenant or contract is a mere convention, an arbitrary instrument emerging out of the struggle for power as a compromise between inflicting injury and suffering injury (under which compromise, whatever is ordered is "lawful and just"); John Locke, on the other hand, held that the contract is an instrument through which the individuals who come together to constitute a political society acknowledge rights that are anterior to the contract itself. The former position is untenable inasmuch as it obviates any real distinction between a just and an unjust order and places the content of the contract beyond the moral scrutiny of those who are bound by the contract. The latter position really declares in so many words that rational beings in the expression of their will to freedom are moved to affirm their *natural rights,* including the right to good government and good laws.[3] A convenant or

1. Plato, *Republic*, 2. 5. 358E-359B.

2. John Locke, *The Second Treatise of Civil Government,* ed. J. W. Gough (Oxford: Basil Blackwell, 1948), chap. 2, p. 5; chap. 9, p. 64.

3. Cf. John Rawls, *A Theory of Justice* (Cambridge, Mass.: Harvard University Press, 1971), p. 11: "My aim is to present a conception of justice which generalizes and carries to a higher level of abstraction the familiar theory of the social contract as found, say, in Locke, Rousseau,

contract in this sense thus points beyond itself to the moral foundation obtaining in the claims of persons. It is with the historic debate about such a "foundation of rights" that the following discussion is concerned.

The *Institutes* of Justinian open with the definition of justice as "the constant and lasting will to give to each man his due."[4] Roman law distinguished between the free man and the slave; it was primarily concerned with the claims of the free individual, that is, the person having a reasonable will, capable of having and being subject to rights, and having capital status (liberty, citizenship, and membership in a family). The rights or claims of free individuals were distinguished as *rights* with respect to persons (*ius personarum*), *rights* with respect to things (*ius rerum*), and *rights* of civil procedure involving property, contract, and injury (*ius actionum*).[5] A right against persons is a claim arising from status or condition, as a right over things is a claim upon the acquisition and use (*dominium*) of goods. The rights of civil procedure, not really a distinct genus of rights, derive from the rights against persons and the rights over things.[6] What is reflected here is essentially Aristotle's scheme of *particular justice*, namely, the justice that pertains to divisible goods and in its branches is distributive, commercial, and remedial.[7] The rights of persons—of individuals invested with titles and subject to obligations—are the claims of free individuals upon the conditions of well-being insofar as these are

---

and Kant. . . . the guiding idea is that the principles of justice for the basic structure of society are the object of the original agreement. They are the principles that free and rational persons concerned to further their own interests would accept in an initial position of equality as defining the fundamental terms of their association."

4. *Corpus Iuris Civilis,* vol. 1, *Institutiones*, ed. Paul Krueger (Berlin, 1877), 1. 1. 3: "Iustitia est constans et perpetua voluntas ius suum cuique tribuens."

5. Ibid., 1. 2. 12; 1. 3; 2. 1; 4. 6. 1.

6. Cf. John Austin, *Lectures on Jurisprudence* (London: John Murray, 1873), 1:41-47, 379-95.

7. Cf. Aristotle, *Nicomachean Ethics,* 5. 2. 12-13; 5. 3; 5. 4.

within the command of society acting with power and authority (*imperium*).

In spite of the limitations of ancient legal thought, in its notions of "person" and "status" there is the clear affirmation that law is a rule of reason which expresses what is good and equal (*ars boni et aequi*). This affirmation is the moral pretension to require of the processes of civil order the preservation of the freedom of the individual. This is in the main the position of medieval and modern writers who carried forward and refined the view that law in idea is both a declaration and a defense of the rights of citizens. This position differs sharply from the view, dominant in the modern world from the time of Hobbes, that law in definition is the will of a sovereign power: law is what is commanded or ordered by any source that can compel obedience.[8] This modern view treats law as a political phenomenon, as an accoutrement of power and an instrument of coercion.[9] If law is necessary to peace and order and if the reasonableness of the law is not a sufficient condition of obedience and orderliness, then the *essence* of law must simply be found in what is sufficient for public quiet, namely force or sanction. This is the line of argument advanced by writers from Hobbes to Kelsen, an argument that does not deny that "good laws" are precisely those which support, in Hobbes' words, "the safety of the people" in "all . . . contentments of life." What is denied is that the "lawful" can have *validity* other than in terms of power or sanction. Considerations of the content of law do not, then, touch or affect the validity of law. And the

8. On the main patterns in European political and legal thought, cf. Michael Oakeshott's introduction to Hobbes' *Leviathan* (Oxford: Basil Blackwell, 1960), p. xii.

9. Cf. A. Passerin d'Entrèves, *Natural Law: An Introduction to Legal Philosophy* (London: Hutchinson's University Library, 1951), pp. 96-97: "The rise of modern jurisprudence is marked by the abandonment of natural law and by a new or 'positive' approach to legal experience. . . . The word 'positivism,' if one cares to use it in this connection, can indicate only an attitude rather than a definite philosophical creed. Indeed the oldest argument against natural justice is the skeptical argument. It goes back to the very beginnings of speculative thought. It has a long history which stretches down from the Sophists to the present day."

intrusion of moral questions upon matters of legitimacy, so goes this argument, can only result in the confusion of moral and legal categories and the hampering of analysis in these separate and distinct realms of investigation.

The difficulty here, as observed in an earlier discussion, is the confusion between *what is ordered* and *what must be obeyed.* Obedience to law is clearly not entailed by command, even if one attempts to hold that 'to be ordered' means simply 'to be compelled to obey'. The precise content of what is commanded is always open to the moral scrutiny of those who are called upon to obey the command, and the presumed nexus between command and obedience disappears entirely with the action of the individual who chooses to defy a command. As command is the act of one will, so disobedience is the act of another will in its independent dissent and opposition.

In the contemporary world, H. L. A. Hart has taken up the matter at this point, contending that what is normative in the realm of law is not the command or sanction of the sovereign power but the validity or legitimacy of the law's enactment.[10] His analysis of law or legal systems reveals elements of two types, namely, *primary rules* and *secondary rules.* Primary rules simply indicate what the law is or what is to be obeyed (that is, what obligations are imposed for doing and forbearing in a given social group) whereas secondary rules indicate what powers are conferred to support these obligations or to modify obligations in one way or another.[11] Among the secondary rules is the ultimate *rule of recognition,* which provides the criteria by which the primary rules of obligation are identified and accepted as valid. This rule of validity is itself neither valid

10. H. L. A. Hart, *The Concept of Law* (Oxford: The Clarendon Press, 1961), pp. 18-79.

11. Ibid., pp. 77-88. Cf. ibid., p. 79: "We shall not indeed claim that wherever the word 'law' is 'properly' used this combination of primary and secondary rules is to be found; for it is clear that the diverse range of cases of which the word 'law' is used are not linked by any such simple uniformity, but by less direct relations. . . . We accord this union of elements a central place because of their explanatory power in elucidating the concepts that constitute the framework of legal thought."

nor invalid but "is simply accepted as appropriate for use in this way."[12]

This approach to the problem of law does not really meet the moral demand of distinguishing just law from what is unjust. What Hart offers are largely technical observations in the place of theoretical considerations, and the substantive questions about justice and fairness are left unanswered. A legal instrument that is recognized or recognizable as having certain "marks" of "legitimacy" is not thereby less subject to review or debate on moral grounds. Procedure in the guise of "secondary rules" is a housekeeping matter, arising from the need to guarantee that the handling of human affairs is not at any point left up to caprice or hazard. Procedure is in this way a part of justice; it cannot, even in the form of a rule of recognition, tell us what justice is. As a theory of law, Hart's position is not significantly different from the tradition that emerges in the modern world with Hobbes, namely, that law in its essence or fundamental character is simply "Will and Artifice" and is accordingly the voice of power rather than the rational expression of authority.

The development of legal thought from Hobbes to John Austin, Hans Kelsen, and H. L. A. Hart is the expression of efforts to distinguish jurisprudence from ethics and sociology and to provide definitions of legal concepts that will be useful in separating law from morality.[13] The importance of this development in the clarification of legal usage, particularly as it affects the formulation of law and the administration of justice, is apparent. Difficulties arise, however, when the question at hand is not *what the law is* or *what the law says* (and means) but whether what the law says is morally tenable or whether the existing or projected law is the best of possible formulations of public policy. It is precisely at this point that the utility of legal positivism or legal analysis, in whatever form, would

12. Ibid., pp. 105-6.

13. Cf. John Austin, *The Province of Jurisprudence Determined,* in *Lectures on Jurisprudence,* 1:81-348. On the different legal positions distinguishable as 'positivistic' or 'analytic', cf. Hart, *The Concept of Law,* pp. 253-54, note (to chap. 9, p. 181) on Legal Positivism.

seem to be exhausted, and one must look elsewhere for answers to substantive questions concerned with the moral foundations of law.

The Search for an Alternative to Positivism

Modern views, divergent from the positivistic and analytic, have sought to give due attention to the content of just law and to the determination of rights in society. These philosophies of law are diverse, having appeared in response to different moral and legal problems. In general, these philosophies have concerned themselves with the *purpose* of the law, examining the moral and social ends with which legislation is involved or to which legislation is to be applied. Paul Vinogradoff, in *Common Sense in Law,* has expressed this approach to law:

> Law aims at right and justice however imperfectly it may achieve this aim in particular cases. . . . If we omitted this attribute from our definition, we should find it very difficult to draw a line between any kind of arbitrary order as to conduct, e.g., the levying of blackmail by a regular association. There must be a certain balance between justice and force in every system of law; and therefore it is impossible to give a definition of law based exclusively on coercion by the State.[14]

To say with Vinogradoff that "law aims at right and justice" is to recognize that law, as an ordering of means to ends, accords with or is at variance with a recognizable moral norm or norms. To this extent, legal investigation is a part of ethics.

For Vinogradoff, law is primarily *volition* rather than *interest* and is defined as a "set of rules imposed and enforced by a society with regard to the attribution and exercise of power

14. Paul Vinogradoff, *Common Sense in Law* (New York: Henry Holt and Company, 1914), p. 42. Cf. W. W. Buchland, *Some Reflections on Jurisprudence* (Cambridge: Cambridge University Press, 1945), p. 33: "No doubt the law does set up in a sense a moral standard and is in the main aiming at right conduct; a view of law which ignores this is misleading. But this is not a reason for including in our definition of law what is not necessarily true of the 'law' with which legal analysis is concerned."

over persons and things."[15] A *right,* accordingly, is "the range of action assigned to a particular will within the social order established by law."[16] Vinogradoff has in mind the agreement of wills brought about by social necessity and supported by force. Into this total legal operation fall both acts of legislation and judge-made (juridical) law, the latter embracing customary law, judicial decisions, and equity.[17] Law for Vinogradoff emerges, in concept, as a determination of rights under the existing conditions of a society as a whole.[18]

The views of Vinogradoff, as representative of "historical jurisprudence,"[19] are not unrelated to the views of those who came to be grouped together under the "sociological school." Both historical and sociological jurisprudence arose out of attention to the demands of social practice and social sentiment (the "living law of people"), together with the singular influence of the writings of Hegel.[20] In sociological jurisprudence, the law is viewed as an ordering of wills and interests, an ordering that gives direction to the "movement" or "social evolution" of a given society.[21] This direction, in the view of Benja-

15. Ibid., p. 59.

16. Ibid., p. 62.

17. Ibid., pp. 116-18.

18. Paul Vinogradoff, *Custom and Right* (Cambridge, Mass.: Harvard University Press, 1925), p. 15: ". . . while law in its own field may work by dialectical analysis, it receives its synthetic impulses from the contents supplied to it by various human activities which are organized and coordinated by it."

19. The "Historical School" of jurisprudence emerged in two branches, in Germany and in England, from the influence of the writings of Friedrich Karl von Savigny.

20. Hegel thinks of law as the reason immanent in organized social existence, i.e., law is an ordering through which the freedom of the individual is actualized. Cf. *Philosophy of Right* trans. T. M. Knox (Oxford: The Clarendon Press, 1962), p. 167: ". . . the genuine truth is . . . the building of reason into the real world. . . . It is by working at this task that civilized man has actually given reason an embodiment in law and government and achieved consciousness of the fact."

21. Cf. W. Friedmann, *Law in a Changing Society* (Berkeley and Los Angeles: University of California Press, 1959), p. 22. Friedmann speaks of ". . . the slowly growing pressure of changed patterns and norms of social

min Cardozo, is essentially a determination of priorities, that is, a movement in "social engineering."[22] The basis of any ordering of wills and interests must be the knowledge gained "from experience and study and reflection; in brief, from life itself."[23]

Cardozo's appeal to "experience, study, and reflection" is made on behalf of "the estimate of the comparative value of one social interest and another when they come, two or more of them, into collision. . . ."[24] The normative character of what is sought by Cardozo is made clear in his saying that he is concerned with "the justice to which law in its making should conform."[25] He is satisfied, accordingly, that sociological jurisprudence without the idea of *natural law* can offer nothing more than "provisional and tentative" proposals as the content of just law. What is involved in Cardozo's view is a certain conjunction of experience and creative insight in a procedure that is objective rather than subjective and tentative. In Cardozo's words:

> The search . . . is for something external, a norm which finds expression in custom or convictions, but, in the very act of declaring what is found, there springs into being a new norm, a new standard, to which custom and convictions tend thereafter to conform.[26]

Cardozo's view of law in its relation to social purpose meets

---

life, creating an increasing gap between the facts of life and the law, to which the latter must ultimately respond."

22. Benjamin Cardozo, *The Growth of the Law* (New Haven: Yale University Press, 1924), pp. 106-7: "An appeal to origins will be futile, their significance perverted unless tested and illumined by an appeal to ends."

23. Benjamin Cardozo, *The Nature of the Judicial Process* (New Haven: Yale University Press, 1921), p. 113.

24. Cardozo, *The Growth of the Law*, p. 85.

25. Ibid., p. 87.

26. Ibid., pp. 95-96. Cf. ibid., p. 87: "Justice in this sense is a concept by far more subtle and indefinite than any that is yielded by mere obedience to a rule. It remains to some extent, when all is said and done, the synonym of an aspiration, a mood of exaltation, a yearning for what is fine or high."

the old moral problem of the ordering of means to ends. To recognize with sociologists that the ordering of human affairs is relative to time and place is not, in fact, to settle any genuine moral or social issues. One faces again and again the problem of determining in what respect, if any, one interest manifesting itself in a society is "higher than" or "prior to" any other interest or interests. There is a sense in which all moral currents in a society are expressions of time and circumstance. What is required is a perception of the propriety of an interest or demand, since propriety is separable from the force or pressure with which an interest or demand is supported and advanced in a particular society. The search for the *purpose* of the law thus involves an appeal beyond social process to objective moral norms, with respect to which competing interests can be assessed and priorities can be determined in any and every ordering of means to end. Cardozo recognizes this fundamental relationship between morality and social justice in his appeal to the "teachings of right reason and conscience"[27] in correction of the limitations of sociological method.[28]

The moral force of concern with the purpose of law, so evident in the writings of Benjamin Cardozo, is manifest in a distinct way in the work of Rudolf Stammler. Stammler's theory of justice is a restatement of Kant's ethics or, rather, an application of the "ethics of the pure will" to the problem of law. For Stammler, ethics and law are concerned with the same subject matter, namely, "the voluntary activities of men," and ultimately go back to the same fundamental law as the highest aim of the will.[29] Law, or just law, is the determination of what is *right* as "the regulation of the social life of man"; the ethical is the commitment of the person in willing what is legally right from a good motive, that is, for its own sake. As opposed to "conventional rules" and "arbitrary commands," the idea of just law involves "a peculiar quality of norms laid down by

27. Cf. Cardozo, *The Nature of the Judicial Process,* p. 137.

28. Cf. Huntington Cairns, *Legal Philosophy from Plato to Hegel* (Baltimore: The Johns Hopkins Press, 1966), pp. 237-41.

29. Rudolf Stammler, *The Theory of Justice*, trans. Isaac Husik (New York: The Macmillan Comapny, 1925), p. 65.

men"; the idea of just law is "a method of determining when the content of specific law is just."[30] The *idea* of law itself has no material content that is distinguishable from the content of a particular law.[31] Concerning the content of particular laws, Stammler says:

> Every rule of external conduct contains two kinds of elements which make up the content of the rule. The one is made up of those elements which constitute this rule a specific thing. . . . The second consists of the intellectual elements of a will content which are necessarily and universally contained in each and every law.[32]

In seeking for the "universal and necessary elements and their fundamental and constructive unity," Stammler avoids all contingent conditions of social life and finds the abstract idea of law in the formula of "a community of men willing freely."[33] This formula, as Stammler believes, comprehends "all possible purposes of persons united under the law."[34] In seeking to bridge the gap between the concept of law and the laws themselves, Stammler offers "principles of just law," which indicate as methodological guides what can be considered the just treatment of persons in the enactment of particular laws, that is, in the ordering of relations in a given community.

The strength of Stammler's position is the insistence that law

30. Ibid., p. 89.
31. Ibid., p. 91.
32. Ibid., p. 133. Cf. ibid., pp. 472-73: "The *concept* of law is preliminary to the problem of its *compulsory character,* and the latter can be established only as a means to the uniformity of social life. Finally, as the latter is always conditioned by *just legal content,* this, as the culminating and dominant point, forms the crown of social study in general and offers the place of union for all investigation of a social condition."
33. Ibid., p. 153.
34. Cf. ibid., p. 157: "The idea of a community of free men is not itself a legal proposition. It is not on the same level with the rule that a debtor must add interest on a delayed payment. . . . In the idea of a just law as defined by the social ideal we are dealing not with the content of a legal proposition but with a formal *method.*"

as an *ordering* is a moral matter, which accords with or fails to accord with the moral norm of the *idea of law.* Thus a precise legal content is morally binding only when this content is consistent with the *form* of just law: the formula of "reciprocal freedom" under which each individual is able to be his own neighbor. Stammler is maintaining that every law, as an ordering of relations in a community, is a pretension to *just law* but that not every law embodies what is just. Accordingly, every statement of *what law is* entails a statement of *what law ought to be.*

Stammler's position affirms that lawmaking is an enterprise occasioned by a social need and governed by a moral norm. This is in direct opposition to the view that *law* can arise from determinations that have as their object merely the exercise and consolidation of power, as, for example, on the part of any individual or individuals seeking to rule for their own interest. Stammler's position offers a "middle way" between holding that every legal order is arbitrary and holding that every legal order is rational and just. In saying that every law makes a pretension to be "just law," Stammler is maintaining that any ordering as such is a relation of means to an end for a community of persons and involves, accordingly, a *deliberate* act in furtherance of the good of that community. To deny Stammler's point would be to hold that one can somehow engage in prescribing means to an end without the recognition, on one's own part or the part of others, that such is indeed an act of *prescribing* in accordance with some aim or some norm of human good. This would make of legislating a grand game of self-deception as well as the deception of others. But to accept Stammler's point would not be to hold that in lawmaking one can prescribe only what is the best means to ends and therefore what is indeed just. In the realm of the normative, there are more or less adequate means to the same end, as there may be means to illusory or mistaken ends or means to ends imperfectly understood. The involvement with ends and means is always an involvement with norms and, in ultimate intention, with *the norm* of human good. In this sense, all lawmaking as well as all deliberate behavior in society must be said to aim at what is just, however defective such lawmaking may in fact be.

The problem that is not fully resolved in Stammler's exposition is that of the character of the norm of justice. The norm of a community of persons willing freely can indeed be understood in terms of "equal justice" as the meaning of "reciprocal freedom." This would require that no individual can express his freedom in a way that is arbitrarily denied to another. But then it must be granted that the norm of just law, the "social ideal," is itself a moral content that is distinguishable from other "ways of ordering" of human affairs. In seeking to separate in just law what is "merely empirical and subject to constant change" from what is invariant,[35] Stammler maintains that the invariant element is a formula of consistency or noncontradiction. Such a formula can be understood as a principle of fairness, inasmuch as one wishes to hold that a rational being cannot propose any scheme of unilateral freedom without involving himself in a contradiction. Unilateral freedom, viewed as a *rule* of conduct—as universal practice—is inconsistent in that its results, by encroaching upon freedom, are incompatible with its aim as the affirmation of freedom. From this it does not follow, however, that reciprocal freedom is nothing but consistency of action. Respect for persons as ends always, as the full meaning of "reciprocal freedom," is a distinct moral content and not merely a formula for bringing order to the variable content of human volition. In seeking to avoid the problem of "validity of content" of the "old law of nature," Stammler appears to ignore the problems arising out of his one "formal method" and to confuse what is sufficient with what is merely necessary in the establishment of a just social order.[36]

Lon Fuller, in more recent times, has sought in a different way to advance a theory of legality and justice as "some variety

35. Ibid., p. 90.

36. Cf. Gustav Radbruch, *Rechtsphilosophie*, 6th ed. (Stuttgart: K. F. Koehler, 1963), p. 117: "Die Lehre vom richtigen Rechte will und kann keinen einzigen Rechtssatz entwickeln, der mit Allgemeingültigheit als richtig erweisen werden könnte. Sie erkauft die Allgemeingültigheit ihrer Begriffe um den Preis ihres rein formalen Charakters. So ist sie weniger eine Rechtsphilosophie als eine Logik der Rechtsphilosophie. . . ."

of natural law."[37] Fuller is concerned more with procedural than with substantive matters and, accordingly, more with a procedural than with a substantive "natural law." He speaks of "the inner morality of law and of the demands of this morality: generality of rules, promulgation, limitation upon retroactive laws, clarity, noncontradiction, avoidance of requiring the impossible, constancy of law in time, and congruence between enacted and administered law.[38]

Fuller holds, further, that law is not simply a phenomenon of social existence, not merely a "manifested fact of social authority or power."[39] The making and administration of law is a purposeful activity. There is a purpose to the law as a whole, namely, "that of subjecting human conduct to the guidance and control of general rules.[40] This is Fuller's "modest indulgence in teleology," yielding a "procedural natural law" which is neutral with respect to many ethical issues but committed to a view of man as "a responsible agent, capable of understanding and following rules, and answerable for his defaults."[41]

But Fuller wants to declare more than this, and so he proposes as the *substantive* aim of the law both the support of community and the support of communication among men as a way of being alive. In Fuller's words:

> If I were asked . . . to discern one central indisputable principle which may be called substantive natural law—Natural Law with capital letters—I would find it in the injunction: Open up, maintain, and preserve the integrity of the channels of communication by which men convey to one another what they perceive, feel and desire."[42]

There is significance in Fuller's recognition that attention to procedure, in the form of a "procedural natural law," involves a

37. Lon L. Fuller, *The Morality of Law*, rev. ed. (New Haven: Yale University Press, 1969), p. 96.
38. Ibid., pp. 33-94.
39. Ibid., p. 145.
40. Ibid., p. 146.
41. Ibid., p. 162. Cf. Lon L. Fuller, *The Law in Quest of Itself* (Chicago: The Foundation Press, 1940), pp. 99-140.
42. Fuller, *The Morality of Law*, p. 186.

commitment to an end or ends that are beyond the procedures themselves. There is at least a tacit recognition of claims, upon community and the channels of communication, as ends of law which go beyond the mere determination of who is to be obeyed by whom and beyond what is required by the grammar and logic of "correct" lawmaking. Fuller thus comes in his own way to a recognition of rights and duties that are anterior to the written laws; insofar as the laws of a society give attention to those rights and duties they can be regarded as *good laws.* Fuller's "modest indulgence in teleology" is an affirmation of an order of law that accords with the rationality and responsibility of individuals who seek to exercise their freedom in an open society.

From Lon Fuller's natural law ideas we turn finally to the theory of political justice found in John Rawls's *A Theory of Justice.* Rawls offers a position which is explicitly a restatement, at "a higher level of abstraction," of 'social contract' views coming down from Hume, Locke, Rousseau, and Kant.[43] This "higher level" is simply the level of the regulative principles of human association, which define the equality of "free and rational persons." This is the level of *justice as fairness.*

The equality that Rawls expounds is the equality of access to primary goods, namely, rights and liberties, powers and opportunities, income and wealth.[44] This is the first of two primary principles of justice. The sense of the first principle carries over to the second, namely, that inequalities are to be permitted only where they are of the greatest benefit to the least advantaged in a society and are attached to stations open to all under conditions of fair equality of opportunity.

Rawls conceives of organized society as a *rational order* under which an individual would choose to forfeit the possibility of having more than others if there are guarantees that he will not have less than others.[45] And under this order, every advan-

43. Rawls, *A Theory of Justice,* p. 11.

44. Ibid., p. 62. Cf. ibid., p. 60.

45. Ibid., pp. 150-51: "Since it is not reasonable . . . to expect more than an equal share in the division of social goods, and since it is not

tage to any given individual, in being of benefit to the least advantaged, must be of benefit to all. In this way, Rawls argues for the recognition of a residual respect for the individual who in his status as a free and rational being and as a citizen is not to be disadvantaged by the social arrangements set by other free and rational beings. This has much of the sound of the traditional view, coming down from Aristotle, that just law is governance that is ordered to the common good.

The device that Rawls employs to advance his view of equality and fairness is the "veil of ignorance" in the "Original Position," in which situation presumably the principles of justice would be decided upon.[46] In the Original Position, the individual is taken to be ignorant of precisely that knowledge about himself that could be exploited so as "to tailor principles to his advantage."[47] In this situation, behind a veil of ignorance, one would choose a system of justice in which moral claims are separated from claims that arise from the accidents of birth (physical and mental endowments or talents) and social position.[48] The individual thus adopts the principles of justice on their own merits as principles of fairness, that is, as principles which stand as *reasonable* when seen from the point of view of the common advantage that embraces the advantage of each. In Rawls's words:

> The natural distribution is neither just nor unjust; nor is it unjust that men are born into society at some particular position. These are simply natural facts. What is just and unjust is the way that institutions deal with these facts. Aristocratic and caste societies are unjust because they make these contingencies the ascriptive basis for belong-

---

rational . . . to agree to less, the sensible thing . . . to do is to acknowledge as the first principle of justice one requiring an equal distribution. Indeed, this principle is so obvious that we would expect it to occur to anyone immediately."

46. Ibid., pp. 136-42.

47. Ibid., p. 139.

48. Ibid., p. 140: ". . . each individual is forced to choose for everyone." Cf. ibid., p. 148: "[the individual] voluntarily takes on the limitations expressed by this interpretation of the moral point of view."

ing to more or less enclosed and privileged social classes. The basic structure of these societies incorporates the arbitrariness found in nature. But there is no necessity for men to resign themselves to these contingencies. The social system is not an unchangeable order beyond human control but a pattern of human action. In justice as fairness men agree to share one another's fate.[49]

One is struck with the resemblance between what Rawls has to say about equality and Kant's idea of "reciprocal freedom." Rawls himself speaks of the Original Position as a "procedural interpretation of Kant's conception of autonomy and the categorical imperative."[50] One imagines that Rawls means to say that in the Original Position individuals, as free and equal rational beings, act so as to establish and support an "ethical commonwealth" as the full expression of their freedom and rationality, that is to say, of their autonomy. This, it would seem, is faithful to the sense of what Kant says about moral autonomy and reciprocal freedom.

Kant holds that freedom of choice (*arbitrium liberum*) is not a sufficient condition of autonomy, although this freedom is a necessary condition of responsibility. Autonomy requires that free and rational beings impose upon themselves an *order* of conduct, not simply adopt interests in accordance with what is pleasant. The scoundrel, in choosing to be a scoundrel, adopts a maxim or takes up a mode of behavior that is incompatible

49. Ibid., p. 102.

50. Ibid., p. 256. Cf. Victor Gourevitch, "Rawls on Justice," *The Review of Metaphysics* 28 (March, 1975):487: "Rawls' 'veil of ignorance' is justice's familiar blindfold. To withdraw behind it is to suspend all reference to one's own and to one's fellows' particular needs, desires, capacities, or beliefs: to everything that sets one person apart from another. The veil thus replaces the natural variety of distinct individuals with so many anonymous, general, and hence interchangeable counters. Since they do not know what might be to their own as against another's advantage once the veil is lifted, it makes no sense for them to bargain about principles of justice. . . . They have no alternative but to 'choose' principles impartially and on their own merits. Under the circumstances anyone's choice is everyone's. Choosing behind the veil of ignorance is Rawls' equivalent of universalization."

with membership in a rational community of equals.[51] It is in membership in such a community that the freedom of noumenal selves is expressed or realized fully. As Kant speaks of what rational beings *should do* in opposition to purposes that are "only subjectively valid and empirical," Rawls speaks of what free and equal rational beings *would do* in ignorance of their particular talents and advantages.

An Esquisse

Reflecting upon the theories that have just been reviewed, one finds as a common element the rejection of the separation of law or legal justice from morality. This separation may be seen as part of the empirical bent of mind, which eschews questions of value as obscure if not unanalyzable matters. One can, perhaps, be more sure of what the law says and what the law ordains than of what makes the law *just* or worthy of obedience. And one may want to say that the separation of legal fact from moral norm is made credible by the existence of diverse standards of morality and justice or by what appears to be the erosion of moral consensus in a society. If there are no moral norms that are recognized by all or most citizens, then the search for the justification of public policy and public practice may well be taken to be a quest for what cannot be found. If the recognition of 'just law' implies a moral community, then the absence of such a community would suggest the abandonment of the idea of just law (*richtiges Recht*) and the substitution of the idea of 'valid law' (*geltendes Recht*). The inadequacy of such substitution, as well as the confusion involved therein, is seen in this passage from H. L. A. Hart's *The Concept of Law:*

> If we narrow our point of view and think only of the person who is called upon to *obey* evil rules, we may regard it as a matter of indifference whether or not he thinks that he is faced with a valid rule of 'law' so long as

51. Cf. Rawls, *A Theory of Justice*, pp. 254-55: Rawls comments on Henry Sidgwick's dissatisfaction with Kant's categorical imperative as the basis for the distinction between the saint as a 'good man' and the scoundrel as a 'bad man'.

> he sees its moral iniquity and does what morality requires. . . . A concept of law which allows the invalidity of law to be distinguished from its immorality, enables us to see the complexity and variety of these separate issues, whereas a narrow concept of law which denies legal validity to iniquitous rules may blind us to them.[52]

Here is the attempt to have it both ways: to recognize that a law may be judged iniquitous and to hold, at the same time, that there are reasons for obeying the same law.

In the opposition to moral and legal skepticism, one must come around, it seems, to the idea of a rule or law as a conforming of human practice to *natural order* or *natural reason.* In considering the senses in which one can speak of the lawful, there is the question whether or not one can speak at all of a 'bad law' or 'unjust law' as a *law.* The problem of any governance or at least of the governance of the modern sovereign state arises from the power to command what is fatuous or oppressive as well as what is reasonable and beneficial. If individuals are required to do what is against their best interests and against their dignity as persons, they are involved with obligations that do not pertain to the exercise of freedom, that is, their freedom in society is compromised by demands and restraints that serve purposes other than the common promotion of their well-being. The compromise of freedom in organized society is analogous if not equivalent to the denial of freedom in the 'state of nature', in which there is the unilateral exercise of liberty in accordance with the advantage or advantages that one individual enjoys, by whatever circumstances, over another individual. The moral complication of regarding unfairness and inequality as lawful is avoided simply in making a distinction between 'what is ordered' and 'what is lawful' and in saying with St. Augustine that "a law that is not just is not a law."

The distinction between the ordered and the lawful undermines, obviously, the contention that resistance to public policy is an attack upon the idea of law or upon the idea of political society as a lawful order. In a more significant way, this

52. Hart, *The Concept of Law*, pp. 206-7.

distinction undermines the claim that *any* ordering is lawful or legitimate. An ordering, as a *rule* for a group of individuals, is really a pretension to what is lawful, a thrust away from the prerogatives (and risks) of liberty toward the commitments and guarantees of reciprocal freedom. While every ordering as *policy* is distinguishable from the volition of a private individual, an ordering as such may fall short of what is lawful in failing to set forth or accord with the commitments and guarantees of free and equal persons. In falling short, an ordering is simply a counterfeit of law and an "order of law" is merely a "public quiet" under which some suffer more injustice and enjoy less liberty than others.

Law as a way of governing or as a body of governance embraces both the procedural (that is, the determining of the law) and the substantive (that is, what is determined as the law). Law as public policy involves the intrusion of a public or general will upon the will of the individual, even when this public will coincides with the intention of the individual. In being ordered to act or to forbear, the individual is confronted with what he must do, as a member of society, as distinct from what he may or may not do according to his own predilection or judgment. As public policy, law must be promulgated and the promulgating source must be recognized as *the* source of law as distinct from all other sources, actual or possible. The voice of the "strong man" or "wise man" or of a legislative body must compete with and prevail over other voices for *recognition* as the source of order and authority in a given community or society.

It is clear, at the same time, that the way in which law is brought forward from its source and received by the governed has nothing to do with what the law says as a precise ordering. The claim that what the prince says is to be obeyed (*quod placuit principi, legis habet vigorem*) reveals nothing about the adequacy of what the prince says or about reasons for obeying the prince rather than the dictates of one's conscience.[53] If one

53. Cf. St. Thomas Aquinas, *Summa Theologiae* First Part of the Second Part, Q. 90, A. 1, trans. Thomas Gilby, O. P. (London: Eyre and Spottiswoode, Ltd., 1966): "To have the quality of law in what is . . .

were to hold that 'promulgation' on the part of a lawgiver and 'acceptance' on the part of the governed gives being and validity to law, one would abstract from all substantive content of what is ordered and give attention solely to the extra-moral facts concerning the resources of power and the responses to power. As a despot may be the source of 'good laws' and an assembly of all citizens may be the source of 'bad laws', the *making of law* does not provide a clue to the character of the law that is made.

The making of law is a distinct kind of ordering that enters into every body of law. The making of law is an ordering that is concerned with ordering and is constitutive therefore of authority and of the offices of authority in society. Inasmuch as law is always governance that confronts the individual in relations of external or public life, the making of law is as much a part of the public life of the individual as is the observance of law. Both making and observing, with respect to law, are demands upon the rationality of any individual who is capable of independent judgment and assent and whose judgment, accordingly, can be neither ignored nor anticipated. This is the point made by Kant, in saying that a rational being as a citizen must have "as much of a moral capacity to bind juridically" another as the other has to bind him.[54] Lawmaking becomes justified as the full participation of citizens in their own governing and being governed.[55]

It should be clear that procedural matters belong to a body of law as part of its content. Legal procedures are means to legal and moral ends, but means that are also ends themselves. Among the rights of free individuals are those pertaining to

---

commanded the will must be ruled by some reason, and the maxim, *the prince's will has the force of law*, has to be understood with that proviso, otherwise his will would make for lawlessness rather than law."

54. Cf. Immanuel Kant, *The Metaphysical Elements of Justice*, trans. John Ladd (Indianapolis: The Bobbs-Merrill Company, Inc., 1965), pp. 78-79.

55. Ibid., p. 78. Kant's position is weakened by the distinction he makes between active and passive citizens, the latter being those who are not fit to vote. Kant includes, in the class of passive citizens, apprentices, servants, and women as lacking "civic personality" (p. 79).

participation in the support of a just legal order. This participation takes two forms, namely, (1) direct or indirect involvement in the formation of law and the establishment of authority (and its agencies) and (2) direct or indirect involvement in the review of law as established. Whether the participation is direct or indirect does not affect the basic democratic principle concerned, namely, that the individual in his rational assent or dissent is the author of or consultant upon the law that he is called upon to obey.[56] This means that the individual must be included, directly or indirectly, in every forum through which law passes, from intention of will to enactment and possibly repeal. Even if it were proposed that a code of law embrace only rules that are divine in origin, it would be necessary to contend therewith that what is revealed as just law is what reason would have devised through a democratic process of lawmaking and review.

The 'rights of participation' in the lawmaking process are simply the rights through the exercise of which arises a *legitimate* order controlling the affairs of free and equal persons. An order that arises or persists in disregard of these rights is, accordingly, *illegitimate.* The legitimacy of a legal order is a *moral* determination, which is separable from and independent of the facts of power and the pretensions to authority.[57] At the same time, it is precisely to legitimacy in this moral sense that an

56. Cf. William Blackstone, *Commentaries on the Laws of England,* 1. 2. 2, ed. St. George Tucker (South Hackensack, N. J.: Rothman Reprints, 1969), 2:158. "In a free state, every man, who is supposed a free agent, ought to be in some measure his own governor; and, therefore, a branch, at least, of the legislative power should reside in the whole body of the people."

57. There is indeed a *science* of law (*Rechtswissenschaft*) which concerns itself with an existing code or codes of law and with the meaning and scope of 'legal statements' appearing in such a code or codes. This science abstracts from all ethical considerations and cannot, therefore, be concerned in a strict sense with legitimacy as a moral matter. Cf. Radbruch, *Rechtsphilosophie*, p. 209: "Diese eigentliche Rechtswissenschaft, die systematische, dogmatische Rechtswissenschaft, kann definert werden als die *Wissenschaft vom objectiven Sinn positiver Rechtsordnungen.* . . . Sie ist Wissenschaft vom geltenden, nicht vom richtigen Recht, vom Rechte, das ist, nicht vom Rechte, das sein sollte."

appeal would be made in any effort to oppose an existing legal order or parts of an order as arbitrary and oppressive. It is inherent in the very meaning of the freedom of a people that they choose through open discussion the laws under which public affairs are to be managed. One may think of the *idea* of a legal code as arising from the idea of a general convention and plebiscite to which a people "summon themselves" for the purpose of instituting a just government.[58]

The rights of participation that are exercised in the formulation of law are indeed exercised in the furtherance of other rights, namely, "rights of access" to the benefits of an organized society. Any catalogue of rights that are legal as well as moral is subject to criticism and rejection as incomplete and sectarian.[59] There is less likelihood of difficulty in this matter if attention is given to kinds or categories of rights, corresponding to the common needs of individuals in society. Blackstone, in his *Commentaries on the Laws of England,* calls attention to the absolute rights of *personal liberty* (freedom of movement and association, freedom from imprisonment or restraint "unless by due course of law"), *personal security* (enjoyment of life, limb, body, health, and reputation), and *private property* (for use, enjoyment, and disposal of acquisitions), and to *auxiliary rights* (e.g., right of parliament, due process, petition, right to bear arms), which support the exercise and enjoyment of absolute rights. These categories are broad enough to stand as the main divisions of a bill of rights of a democratic constitu-

58. Cf. Kant, *The Metaphysical Elements of Justice*, pp. 112-13: "The forms of the state are, as it were, only the *letter* (*littera*) of the original legislation in civil society, and they may therefore continue as long as they are held by ancient, long-standing custom (hence only subjectively) to be necessary to the machinery of the constitution of the state. . . . [The] republican constitution is the only enduring political constitution in which the law is autonomous and is not annexed to any particular person. It is the ultimate end of all public Law and the only condition under which each person receives his due preemptorily. . . . Every true republic is and can be nothing else than a representative system of the people if it is to protect the rights of its citizens in the name of the people."

59. Cf. A. C. Ewing, *Second Thoughts on Moral Philosophy* (London: Routledge and Kegan Paul, Ltd., 1959), pp. 127-34.

tion.[60] Although Blackstone speaks at times of these rights as "inherent in every Englishman," he speaks also of these rights as "inherent by nature in every individual."

The problem of just law is ultimately the problem of equality among individuals in demanding the fulfillment of their purposes. The point is made in Plato's *Republic* that individuals are not equal in native endowment and are not therefore naturally disposed to perform the same functions or to make equal contributions to the common good. This point may be expanded into the view that talent (together with performance) is properly the basis of inequality of claims and inequality of benefits among individuals who are at the same time equal as citizens. It should be clear that the argument in the *Republic* is offered merely to justify diversity of function and division of labor in a complex culture, and to propose the location of individuals in the functions for which severally they are suited. It is not an argument for unequal rewards in accordance with the facts of human inequality or for the subordination of one class of citizens to another through the authority of the state.[61]

The "equal protection of the laws" to which individuals can lay claim would seem to rest upon their status as persons and upon their interdependence as citizens of the same organized society. Whatever his beliefs about and confidence in his own talents and powers, an individual has an awareness of his insufficiency to achieve through solitary effort that good which he holds to be complete. To be an individual is to be aware at once of the importance of one's own interests and needs *and* of the hindrances involved in pursuing these interests without the support of others. In the lack of self-sufficiency no individual is less dependent upon common effort than another individual. This dependence in its precise nature is not affected by the character of the contribution that the individual is able to make to the "common effort" and "common good." Indeed, every contribution, whatever its character, presupposes other contributions as constituents of an adequate and workable order of

60. Blackstone, *Commentaries on the Laws of England,* 1. 1. 1-5.
61. Plato, *Republic*, 519E–520A.

activity.[62] To argue for unequal status and unequal benefit in society on the basis of the unequal contributions that are made to collective enterprise is to confuse the condition of individuals *in society* with some imagined condition of singular, independent beings making social claims in accordance with their estimates of their own merit. The notions of function and of the comparative merit or "weight" of functions is clearly subordinate to the primary intention or thrust of common effort to provide goods and services that can only be obtained through common effort.

The recognition of the rights of citizens and the equal protection of the laws involved therein means simply that social resources must be extended to all persons as social equals. This does not mean, of course, that all individuals are likely to make use or good use of the social resources available to them. One has in mind that the claims of persons upon social resources cannot be treated such that the law becomes an instrument of one person's subjection to another. In the determination of the rational and legal limit of the exercise of any right, discussion would set out from each individual's recognition of the injury or deprivation that he would not wish to endure himself through the free exercise of the powers of others. From this recognition there can emerge and operate in every situation of public judgment a working understanding of the opportunities of freedom and of the restraints upon freedom that individuals, through the law, must impose upon themselves.

While the matter of equality under law is of course broader than the problem of the distribution of external goods, it is clear that many of the most difficult issues of social order stem from the dissatisfaction of citizens with the shares of goods that they receive *vis-à-vis* the shares received by others. There is

62. Cf. G. W. F. Hegel, *Philosophy of Right*, pp. 109-10: ". . . in this identity of the universal will with the particular will, right and duty coalesce, and by being in the ethical order a man has rights in so far as he has duties, and duties in so far as he has rights. In the sphere of abstract right, I have the right and another has the corresponding duty. In the moral sphere, the right of my private judgment and will, as well as of my happiness, has not, but only ought to have, coalesced with duties and become objective."

the conviction in many places that inequality in distribution, in accordance with unequal claims such as merit and inheritance, has a prima facie credibility and that what runs counter to good reason is the proposal of equality of distribution. The tables can be reversed, however: it may be held that equality is the credible state of affairs, particularly in a democratic society, and that what runs counter to our sense of fairness is inequality in distribution. The question that must be answered, in this reversal of the tables, is not why citizens should have the same share of goods according to need but rather why some individuals should have more (or less) than others without regard to need.

It is certainly reasonable for an individual to demand sufficient goods for physical comfort, for the sake of the cultivation of his talents, and for meeting the requirements of leisure and sociability. The goods not acquired or produced by solitary effort must be obtained by one individual through labors with others, through donations, or through the exchange of one thing for another. Aside from the initial advantage of acquisition or seizure (*occupatio*) and the productive exertions of singular effort, the differences in possessions would seem to arise from the relative advantage (or disadvantage) of individuals in the exchange of goods. Fairness of exchange is a primary moral concern inasmuch as the *end* of exchange is presumably, for all parties, the acquisition and use of what is necessary for living well.

Fairness of exchange calls for a body of legislation that would rule out economic practices having the effects of depriving an individual of a "fair share" of goods and of treating him as a "means merely" to the advantage and comfort of others. In terms of human need, as Aristotle observed long ago, an individual can have too little of what is desirable and too much of what is harmful (and, accordingly, too much of what is desirable and too little of what is harmful). What is sought, in moral terms, is a *mean* between extremes in having and not having, this mean being a human condition that is entirely in keeping with the judgment of common sense that an individual should have what he needs and what he can make use of without waste and without depriving others.

5 Power and Punishment

Introduction

Hobbes says in the *Leviathan* that in man's "natural condition" every individual "has a right to every thing; even to one another's body."[1] We know, of course, that this cannot be true or at least that this cannot be accepted as it stands. If conditions were such that each individual had to depend for his safety entirely upon his own resources, it would *not* be true that an individual would have a "right to every thing." The necessity of defending oneself can involve only the right to one's life and safety. And the *right* to one's life can have no meaning if there is a countervailing right against one's life by virtue of another individual's right to everything. A human situation or "natural condition" without established laws and restraints would involve the same "moral" demands of regard for the life of the individual as would a situation with established laws and effective sanctions of peace and order. Contrary to what Hobbes holds, the laws of an established order do not "set in place" the distinction between just and unjust that is the sure alternative to the condition of "the war of all against all."[2] Justice presumably is as ancient as the moral conscience of man. What Hobbes

1. Thomas Hobbes, *Leviathan*, ed. Michael Oakeshott (Oxford: Basil Blackwell, 1960), chap. 14, p. 85.

2. Ibid., chap. 15.

does makes clear, in spite of the general confusion of his position, is that there is an inalienable and indefeasible right to life and safety which is morally anterior to the guarantees of any social agreement or compact.

If all lawgiving may be thought to find its moral justification in the public beneficence that supports the best life of the individual, then the part of law that is concerned with offenses or injuries must be informed with the same beneficence. Public order is simply the order of law, which free individuals impose upon themselves in order to obtain and to hold secure the things that pertain to their well-being. There is a common responsibility for public order, under which responsibility the individual, in not being indifferent to an invasion of his own rights, cannot be indifferent to the invasions of the rights of others. This suggests two principles of the remedy of wrongdoing, namely, (1) that the remedy of wrongdoing must conform to the preservation of the rights of all of the persons of the community, those who offend as well as those offended against, and (2) that the devices of remedy must be such as make *restitution* to those offended against with the least necessary privation of the freedom and dignity of those who offend.

J. S. Mill, in *Utilitarianism,* speaks of "the sentiment of justice" in these words:

> . . . the two essential ingredients in the sentiment of justice are, the desire to punish a person who has done harm, and the knowledge or belief that there is some definite individual or individuals to whom harm has been done. . . . The sentiment of justice, in that one of its elements which consists of the desire to punish, is thus, I conceive, the natural feeling of retaliation or vengeance, rendered by intellect and sympathy applicable to those injuries, that is, to those hurts which wound us through, or in common with, society at large. This sentiment, in itself, has nothing moral in it; what is moral is the exclusive subordination of it to the social sympathies, so as to wait on and obey their call.[3]

3. J. S. Mill, *Utilitarianism*, chap. 5, in *The Utilitarians* (Garden City: Dolphin Books, 1961), pp. 456-57.

Whether or not one agrees with Mill concerning the existence of a "natural feeling of retaliation," it would doubtless be allowed, in conjunction with the recognition of the rights of persons, that there is a sense or sentiment of justice that holds an offender accountable for what he does.[4] The moral question concerns, then, the nature of the remedy of wrongdoing or injury rather than the necessity of remedy.

It has been accepted, in modern times at least, that remedy or punishment, particularly as the satisfaction of major offenses, is an affair of the people acting as a whole—that is, an affair of the state. Remedy or punishment must, accordingly, take a form or forms different from and extending beyond the direct compensation of the injured party. This view reflects the recognition that certain wrongs are indeed grave or heinous and that it is necessary to make a distinction, as in Anglo-Saxon law, between *botless* and *emendable* offenses.[5] In the very notion of a felony there is the idea of punishment as the forfeiture of *status* (as well as property) through imprisonment, torture, banishment, or death.[6] Inasmuch as such penalties do not involve restitution to the injured party or parties, the arguments in support or justification of these penalties must be reviewed

4. Cf. ibid., p. 455: "Justice implies something which is not only the right to do, and wrong not to do, but which some individual person can claim from us as his moral right." In this connection, Aristotle has distinguished three kinds of injury, namely, what is unintentional and unavoidable (ἀτύχημα), what is unintentional and avoidable (ἁμάρτημα), and what is intentional (ἀδίκημα). *Nicomachean Ethics,* 5. 8. 6.

5. Cf. T. F. T. Plucknett, *A Concise History of the Common Law,* 5th ed. (Boston: Little, Brown and Company, 1956), p. 423: ". . . Anglo-Saxon proceedings consequent upon a murder, maiming, theft or serious outrage had little to do with the Crown and were conducted entirely by the party aggrieved; they might result in a punishment, but their principal element was undoubtedly compensation or restitution. Their main characteristic was thus analogous to that of a modern action in tort. Later on, the Crown took a much larger part in such proceedings, and so it is quite plausible to argue that the original stem was mainly tort, and that crime branched off from it."

6. For a brief history of criminal law thought, cf. Helen Silving, *Criminal Justice* (Rio Piedras, Puerto Rico: University of Puerto Rico Press, 1971), 1:69-144.

in a continuing discussion concerning the rights and duties of individuals in society.

Punishment is either nonrestitutive or restitutive.[7] Punishment as nonrestitutive has been justified chiefly in three ways, namely, (1) as the retaliation of suffering upon the wrongdoer; (2) as a means of the moral instruction or correction of the offender; and (3) as a means of deterring the offender and others from further wrongdoing. In the first of these, attention is given to what an individual deserves to suffer for a voluntary act that is wrong or wicked; in the second, the concern is chiefly pedagogic or corrective; in the third, the attention is upon the protection of the members of society at large through the prevention of wrongdoing. It is clear, of course, that these alternative views of punishment are not mutually exclusive and that the punishment of offenders may be justified on more than one ground. It is also clear that there may be confusion in the moralist's or jurist's mind as to precisely which view of punishment he is espousing and as to the bearing of his position on the remedy of precise offenses against precise individuals or groups of individuals.[8]

Punishment as Retaliation or Countersuffering

The moral justification of *retaliation* rests on the presumed duty to punish those who transgress in their actions the laws of their community. It is held, of course, that the wrongdoer is aware of the moral demands upon him as a citizen and that he acts deliberately in violation of these demands. The wrongdoer has a guilty mind (*mens rea*). Punishment accordingly is a balancing, a making equal (*talio, retributio*), a compelling of the individual to suffer in ratio to the injury that he has inflicted upon another. A civil and humane order is one in which every offense against human life must be satisfied; no wrongdoing can be condoned. And the individual must directly atone for

7. The Latin *poena* has the sense of compensation as well as vengeance and suffering.

8. On the distinction between *aim* and *justification* of punishment, cf. Alf Ross, *On Guilt, Responsibility and Punishment* (Berkeley and Los Angeles: University of California Press, 1975), pp. 60-66.

his action, that is, he must take upon himself his wrongdoing simply because it is *his* wrongdoing (*quia peccatum est*). In the distinctive statement of this position, embracing a defense of the death penalty, Kant speaks of retribution as what is entailed in the committing of a "punishable action" by a member of "the civil union."[9] To ignore punishment, or to permit an individual to escape punishment, would be to contribute to the dissolution of civil society and to the return to the state of nature or violence.[10] The justification of retaliation rests in the preservation of civil society as a moral order, through rendering to each offender what is his due.

There is unclarity as to what is meant in holding that the wrongdoer must "pay for his crime" through suffering in like measure what he as inflicted upon another. There is the difficulty of knowing in what way the suffering of the offender is equal to that of the victim. The punishment conventionally meted out, such as incarceration in a case of mayhem or violent assault, is clearly not equal to or even analogous to the suffering or deprivation of the injured person. Even if one thinks of requiring literally "a limb for a limb," the suffering of the wrongdoer would be different from the suffering of the victim, as the suffering of the guilty is different from the suffering of the innocent. And if perchance, in atoning for an offense, one individual could suffer precisely as another has suffered, no principle of *remedy* of wrongdoing would be established thereby. There would remain the immediate and pressing need to make restitution to the individual whose loss has upset in some way the balance of his life. If the preservation of civil society as a moral order requires public reproof for wrongdoing, this reproof can take a form or forms that direct the atoning efforts of the offender toward the compensation of the victim.[11]

9. Immanuel Kant, *The Metaphysical Elements of Justice,* trans. John Ladd (Indianapolis: The Bobbs-Merrill Company, Inc., 1965), p. 105. Cf. ibid., pp. 101-6.

10. Cf. ibid., p. 100: "If legal justice perishes, then it is no longer worth while for men to remain alive on this earth."

11. One does not ignore the necessity of restraining, in one way or another, the intractable or incorrigible individual. Wrongfulness, as delib-

Punishment as Correction

Not unrelated to the justification of punishment as counter-suffering is the view that recognizes the bearing of punishment upon the moral instruction and correction of offenders. This view draws support from any conception of law and justice that reflects the interest, as expressed by Aristotle, "to make others better through discipline" (*δι' ἐπιμελείας βελτίους ποιεῖν*).[12] This interest carries with it the necessity of devoting care to others in reproving and correcting as well as guiding.[13] This raises the question of the bearing of correction, in whatever form, upon what may be called the "moral improvement" of wrongdoers. Presumably, correction as a device of moral improvement would be effective in arousing or sharpening an offender's sense of fairness in human relationships and in bringing his attention to actions and patterns of actions that are destructive of the good of one or more individuals. This would require not only that the offender recognize the wrong action (with its consequences) as *his* action but also that the recognition be accompanied with or followed by a feeling of regret or grief (*contritio*).

Insofar as the wrongdoer's awareness of the character of his action involves regret or remorse, there is clearly no need of punishment, if the justification of punishment is its bearing upon the moral enlightenment or moral regeneration of the offender. Those who are committed to punishment for the sake of moral correction and improvement are faced, then, with the problem of distinguishing the contrite individual from the uncontrite, in order that public resources not be expended upon the application of correctional procedures where they are not

erate and voluntary behavior, must not however be confused with intractability or depravity. It is only voluntary action which involves an individual with demands for remedy of injury to others.

12. Aristotle, *Nicomachean Ethics,* 10. 9. 17.

13. Ibid., 10. 9. 9.: ". . . we shall need laws to regulate the discipline of adults . . . and in fact the whole life of the people generally; for the many are more amenable to compulsion and punishment than to reason and to moral ideals." Trans. H. Rackham (Cambridge Mass.: Harvard University Press, 1934).

needed. And there arises the further question of the efficacy of correctional measures upon the uncontrite individual.

It would be argued, in support of public correction, that sensitivity to and regret over wrongdoing can be provoked through the disgrace, inconvenience, or severity of punishment; and that the individual offender is clearly benefited, and society as well, insofar as such regret over his action brings him to a resolve to eschew thereafter all wrongdoing.

Doubtless many individuals have been brought to regret their actions through, if not entirely because of, the disgrace, inconvenience, or severity of punishment. The important question for public policy and practice is whether such efficacy of punishment can be determined in any way that would constitute a justification of public correction, that is, whether moral sensititivy and contrition, which are matters of consciousness or inwardness, can be monitored through the relations between penal officers and offenders. And if it is believed that the moral improvement of wrongdoers can be overseen by public officials, it would seem that the character and duration of correction should accord with the offender's need for moral improvement rather than with the character and enormity of the offense. It is not unlikely that one individual's regret over a frightful deed would be morally rehabilitative in a more thorough way and in a briefer time than the regret or grief of another individual whose wrongdoing is less frightful. This, accordingly, would require the judgment of moralists or moral theologians rather than penal functionaries and would require facilities of rehabilitation other than those common in penal practice.

Punishment as Deterrence

Related to the notion of correction is the view that seeks to justify punishment in terms of its efficacy or presumed efficacy in deterring individuals from wrongdoing. The notion of punishment as a deterrent from destructive or otherwise undesirable behavior accords entirely with any moral position that regards the promotion of the safety of every member of society to be a matter of public forethought as well as afterthought and remedy.[14] The deterrent force of punishment is the operation of the *dread of punishment* against any impulse or thrust to wrongdoing. Bentham expresses this view of punishment, as one among many "uses" of punishment, in these words:

> The immediate principal end of punishment is to control action. This action is either that of the offender or of others: that of the offender it controls by its influence, either in his will, in which case it is said to operate in the way of *reformation;* or on his physical power, in which case it is said to operate by *disablement:* that of others it can influence no otherwise than by its influence over their wills; in which case it is said to operate by way of *example.*[15]

And in another passage:

> A punishment may be said to be calculated to answer the purpose of a moral lesson when, by reason of the ignominy it stamps upon the offense, it is calculated to inspire the public with sentiments of aversion toward those pernicious habits and dispositions with which the offense appears to be connected.[16]

14. Cf. Jeremy Bentham, *An Introduction to the Principles of Morals and Legislation* (New York: Hafner Publishing Company, 1948), p. 178: ". . . [the legislator's] first, and most extensive, and eligible object, is to prevent, in so far as it is possible, and worth while, all sorts of offenses whatsoever; in other words, so to manage, that no offense whatsoever may be committed."

15. Ibid., p. 170n.

16. Cf. Cesare Beccaria, *On Crimes and Punishments*, trans. Henry Paolucci (Indianapolis: The Bobbs-Merrill Company, Inc., 1963), p. 42: "The purpose [of punishment] can only be to prevent the criminal from inflicting new injuries on . . . citizens and to deter others from similar acts." See also Jeremy Bentham, *Principles of Penal Law,* in *The Works of Jeremy Bentham,* ed. John Bowring (New York: Russell and Russell, Inc., 1962), 1:396: "General prevention ought to be the chief end of punishment, as it is its justification. . . . when we consider that an unpunished crime leaves the path of crime open, not only to the same delinquent but also to all those who have the same motives and opportunities for entering upon it, we perceive that the punishment inflicted on the individual becomes a source of security to all."

The idea of deterrence brings to mind again Aristotle's conception of the broad moral function of the laws, namely, that good laws support the formation of traits of character that, as constituents of the life in accordance with excellence, are beneficial to the individual and to the community as a whole.[17] Viewed in this way, one may say that every good law deters an individual from foolish and often harmful behavior insofar as the individual, by virtue of the law's moral appeal, is disposed to act as the law requires. The deterrence of law is *positive* where the law's intrinsic moral appeal guides the individual to what is beneficial and away from what is harmful in action. Where the disposition to avoid wrongdoing involves the dread of punishment or public opprobrium, the deterrence of the law is *negative* or punitive. The distinction between the positive and negative deterrence of law is difficult to draw, inasmuch as all laws as public rules are attended with sanctions and penalties. There is a significant difference, nevertheless, between what the individual under legal governance is prompted to do or not to do and what he is afraid to do or not to do.

Concerning the negative deterrence of the laws through the fear or dread of punishment, difficulties arise with (1) the consideration of the presumed effectiveness of punishment, in idea or in practice, in deterring individuals from wrongdoing and with (2) the consideration of the probable dangers to which deterrence, as public policy, exposes all of the members of society. On the first matter, it is recognized that the fear or dread of punishment may deter from offense without the actual inflicting of penalty or punishment upon any individual. It is conceivable that the mere establishment of penalties for offenses, together with the necessary sanctions of enforcement, would be sufficient in a given community to deter all of its members from injuring one another. If there existed a com-

17. Cf. Aristotle, *Nicomachean Ethics,* 10. 9. 8: "And it is difficult to obtain a right education in virtue from youth up without being brought up under right laws; for to live temperately and hardily is not pleasant to most men, especially when young; hence the nurture and exercises of the young should be regulated by law, since temperance and hardiness will not be painful when they have become habitual."

munity without wrongdoing, one might dare to claim that this state of affairs obtained as a direct consequence of the "sentiments of aversion" aroused by the knowledge of the penalties to be imposed upon offenders. But there would be no way of supporting such a claim.

Whatever the possible deterrent effect of the fear and dread of punishment (whether or not actual punishment is carried out), one can always think of other deterrents, including the abhorrence of what is wrongful as such, which may be responsible for an individual's refraining from abuses of one sort or another. One can allow that the fear or dread of punishment does indeed deter many individuals from committing offenses, without allowing that such evidence constitutes the justification or vindication of punishment. We know, of course, that impressive numbers of individuals are *not* deterred from wrongdoing, even from committing those offenses which are punishable by severe or extreme measures. Apparently, with many individuals, the impulse to misconduct lies beyond the reach of the threat of retribution, as with other individuals the impulse to proper conduct asserts itself without the additional spur of public sanctions. It can be said, therefore, that the absence of "deterring measures" can be entertained without the thought of subverting moral restraint or encouraging lawlessness in a broad way.

We must say something next about the difficulty that lies in the danger to which a policy of deterrence exposes the members of a society at the same time that such a policy is advanced as beneficial to the community as a whole. This danger is connected with deterrence as involving behavior in the future rather than in the past.[18] Under the idea of deterrence, a particular punishment can be made to bear an element that is beyond what would be an accounting of the wrongdoer for *what he has done.*[19] This point would be obviated or weakened

18. Cf. Hugo Adam Bedau, "A World Without Punishment? ", in *Punishment and Human Rights,* ed. Milton Goldinger (Cambridge, Mass.: Schenkman Publishing Company, 1974), p. 159.

19. Cf. John Locke, *The Second Treatise of Civil Government,* ed. J. W. Gough (Oxford: Basil Blackwell, 1948), chap. 2, p. 8: "Every transgression may be punished to that degree and with so much severity, as

by the contention that what is primary in deterrence is the *fear* or *dread* of punishment and not the actual carrying out of any precise penalty. But those who think in terms of deterrence would not deny that a determinate punishment is something that *could* be carried out and that the carrying out of a punishment, if only rarely, would contribute to the dread that presumably deters most individuals from wrongdoing. The point is that a punishment, as something to be imposed upon a particular offender, may as a *deterrent* go beyond what is appropriate to the offense. And, by the same token, what is believed to deter from wrongdoing may be extended as punishment to persons who are not offenders.

In any combining of punishment and deterrence in public policy, there is the chance that what is demanded as punishment will reflect a concern with the prevention of wrongdoing that obscures a concern with a particular wrongdoer and *his* offense. If, as Bentham says, the "most eligible object" of the legislator in establishing punishments is to prevent "all sorts of offenses whatsoever,"[20] it may be believed that severe and arbitrary measures are justified as appropriate to this end.[21] There may be the effort to "make an example" of the offender or of any person offered as an offender, an effort which in claiming to serve the interests of the community may well endanger the freedom of the individual. This point is made by Kant in his rejection of any view of punishment that ignores the rights of the offender, that is to say, any view that treats the wrongdoer as a means merely. In Kant's words:

> Judicial punishment can never be used merely as a means to promote some other good for the criminal himself or for society, but instead it must in all cases be imposed on him only on the ground that he has committed a crime;

---

will suffice to make it an ill bargain to the offender, give him cause to repent, and terrify others from doing the like."

20. Cf. Bentham, *An Introduction to the Principles of Morals and Legislation*, p. 178.

21. Cesare Beccaria is careful to declare that only those punishments should be chosen which "will make the strongest and most lasting impression on the minds of men, and inflict the least torment on the body of the criminal." *On Crimes and Punishments,* p. 42.

> for a human being can never be manipulated merely as a means to the purposes of someone else. . . . His innate personality [that is, his right as a person] protects him against such treatment. He must first be found to be deserving of punishment before any consideration be given to the utility of this punishment for himself or for his fellow citizens.[22]

What is important is the distinction between what an individual in fact has done as an offense and what this individual or some other person may do in the future. It is clear that there can be deterrence without punishment. There are apparently many ways through which individuals can be turned away or prevented from committing offenses against others.[23] Although punishment or the dread of punishment may deter from wrongdoing, possible or probable deterrence can never be offered as *justification* for punishment as public policy. Insofar as an individual is responsible for what he has done and for the injurious consequences deriving therefrom, *there* is sufficient reason for *punishing* that individual, that is, for requiring him to answer in some way for his action. To require anything of an offender for any other reason would be to use him "as a means merely," to use him in a way which is not compatible with his status and rights as a person. At the same time, in this sort of thinking the door is opened to other ways in which the wrongdoer or any other individual can be used as a means merely to some end or ends projected by those who make laws.

Punishment as Restitution or Restoration

In the *Nicomachean Ethics,* Aristotle speaks of corrective justice (*τὸ διορθωτικόν*) as that type of justice which applies to

22. Kant, *The Metaphysical Elements of Justice,* p. 100. Cf. Immanuel Kant, *The Critique of Practical Reason,* trans. Lewis White Beck (Indianapolis: The Bobbs-Merrill Company, Inc., 1956), pp. 39-40.

23. With respect to deterrence and prevention, it is important to note that deterrence involves a reason or reasons for desisting from wrongdoing whereas prevention is the explicit hindering of an individual from acting. On the distinction between deterrence and the prevention of crime, cf. Bedau, "A World Without Punishment? ", p. 156.

private transactions, both voluntary and involuntary, and which seeks to restore what has been lost by a victim of wrongdoing.[24] The principle that obtains here is simply that of arithmetical equality, which abstracts from the merit or status of the individuals concerned and "looks only at the nature of the damage, treating the parties as equal." Corrective justice rectifies the imbalance introduced by wrongdoing and thus restores the prior mean (for both parties) between gain and loss. In involuntary transactions, which do not involve contract or agreement—such as theft or murder—the mean between gain and loss is restored "in a sense," that is, not *strictly* as in voluntary transactions but *virtually* or in principle.

Aristotle's idea of corrective or remedial justice provides a basis of determining what a wrongdoer owes to those whom he has injured. Aristotle is aware, of course, that corrective justice cannot be viewed as the whole of a society's defense of its members. Punishment cannot carry the full weight of the need "to mould aright the character of any and every person." There is, then, a significant difference between punishment and social protection, a difference often ignored by those who think of punishment primarily as *the* instrument of reform or deterrence.[25]

The interest in punishment as restitution has a certain connection with the concern to make punishment both more precise and more humane, a concern which in modern times is manifest especially in the writing of Cesare Beccaria. Beccaria holds the view that the "true measure of crime is—namely, the *harm done to society.*"[26] This includes harm against society itself, against the life, goods, or honor of private citizens, and against public morality.[27] Beccaria argues that punishment should be the least necessary, should be proportionate to the crime, and should be the least injurious to the offender. All

24. Aristotle, *Nicomachean Ethics,* 5. 2. 12-13, 5. 4. 3-6, 5. 5. 1-2.

25. Cf. Helen Silving, " 'Rule of Law' in Criminal Justice," in *Essays in Criminal Science,* ed. Gerhard O. Mueller (South Hackensack, N. J.: F. B. Rothman, 1961), pp. 98ff.

26. Beccaria, *On Crimes and Punishments,* p. 64.

27. Ibid., p. 66.

other punishment is useless and tyrannical. Whether in supporting temporary servitude (as a punishment for theft) or protracted servitude (as a substitute for the death penalty), Beccaria is concerned that punishment's "effect on the human spirit," that is, the effect of deterring from wrongdoing, shall be in keeping with what is reasonable, just, and humane. There is confusion, of course, in tying what is thought of as just and humane punishment to what is thought of as effective in deterring from harmful action. Beccaria cannot have it both ways. If punishment is to be just and humane, this can be achieved without concern about deterrence; if punishment is to deter, this can be achieved or attempted without direct concern with what is just and humane. Beccaria appears to recognize this in speaking about harmful action that does not involve a "guilty mind," namely, innocent bankruptcy and light fault, in which there is concern only with *restitution.*[28]

Bentham, who recognized a debt to Beccaria, observed that an act cannot be considered detrimental to a community if it is not "detrimental to some one or more of the individuals that comprise it." Offense or wrongdoing is, in its very character as an offense, a detriment to individuals, whether as distinguishable persons or as "an unassignable indefinite multitude."[29] Bentham's attention to wrongdoing as detriment to the individual is, of course, compatible with the idea of punishment as restitution to the individual. And inasmuch as Bentham speaks of all punishment as "mischief" and in itself evil, it can be argued along Bentham's lines that the "mischief" of punishment could be kept at a minimum through "penalties" of restitution or reparation. Bentham did not ignore restitution but regarded it as a subordinate end of punishment, as applicable only to private offenses, that is, "offenses against assignable *individuals*"[30] and inferior to the control, through example, of the wills of the members of society at large.[31] We have spoken

28. Ibid., p. 77, including note.

29. Bentham, *An Introduction to the Principles of Morals and Legislation,* p. 207.

30. Ibid., p. 302-3.

31. Ibid., p. 170n.

of the difficulties involved in Bentham's idea of deterrence. It is sufficient to say here that the interest of Beccaria and Bentham, in making punishment more precise and more humane, would seem to move in the direction of demanding of wrongdoers only what is in restitution of injuries that they have caused.

The idea of punishment as restitution is the idea of retribution without "countersuffering," for punishment is without injury to the offender for the act of wrongdoing itself. The notion of restitution (*restitutio*) was given a classic statement by St. Thomas Aquinas, in terms applicable to the modern as well as the medieval world. St. Thomas thinks of restitution as an act of commutative justice, an act whose purpose is "to remove the loss from someone from whom a thing has been unjustly taken."[32] The primary concern is with the well-being of the injured party and with the offender's restoration of what has been lost through his wrongdoing, although St. Thomas does allow that in some cases an offense cannot be counterbalanced simply by restitution (*major est actio quam esset passio si sibi sola res illa auferretur*[33]).

For St. Thomas, as for Aristotle, the injuries that are covered by commutative justice involve transactions or exchanges (*commutationes*) that are both voluntary (with consent) and involuntary (without consent). Under these headings fall all injuries of individuals with respect to their property, their persons (life, health, dignity), and their work. In each case, the concern of justice must be to compensate the one who is de-

32. St. Thomas Aquinas, *Summa Theologiae,* Second Part of the Second Part, Q. 62, A. 6, trans. Thomas Gilby, O. P. (London: Eyre and Spottiswoode, Ltd., 1975).

33. Ibid., Q. 61, A. 4. Cf. ibid., Q 62, A. 3: "Two consequences follow when another's property is unjustly taken. One is the displacement of the balance respecting the property; . . . The other is the fault of injustice, and this may not amount to upsetting the objective balance of things, as when someone intends to inflict violence but does not succeed. . . . As for the second, the remedy is applied by punishment, the imposition of which is for a judge." This 'second remedy' is retaliation or 'countersuffering' (*contrapassum*). For St. Thomas, commutative justice is the larger thing, of which restitution is a part.

prived or injured in some way, through reparation by the offender and his accomplices. In the words of St. Thomas:

> Restitution redresses the balance of commutative justice, which consists . . . in the equalizing of things. This cannot be done unless what is lacking is made up to one who has less than his due. To supply this lack restitution must be made to the one from whom something has been taken.[34]

> Whoever brings loss upon another, it seems, takes from him that to which it amounts. . . . That is why a man is bound to make restitution for the loss he has brought upon another.[35]

The position taken by St. Thomas is entirely in accordance with fairness and with the moral inclination of many members of a group or society. Quite apart from the sanction of public authority, it is reasonable and fitting for an individual to make restitution in some form for injury or insult to another person. The "disposition to restore" manifests itself countless times in relations or transactions between friends and between strangers, where there has been injury *without* the intention to harm. Matters are different, of course, under other circumstances. But even the intention to harm, which makes injurious action blameworthy and villainous, does not overturn the *fittingness* of restitution or undermine the sense of what is right in particular situations of injury. The "intention to harm" and the "disposition to restore" are opposing inclinations which can be bridged through the contrition of the injuring party. A bridge is also made through public authority in the general requirement and expectation that a citizen accept responsibility for his actions and their consequences. In its broad scope, restitution includes remedies not only for injuries to precise individuals but also for offenses against the welfare of each and every individual, that is, abuses against the common weal (*utilitas publica*), reckoned as common property and common freedom. Restitution as individual determination or social policy

34. Ibid., Q. 62, A. 5. Cf. ibid., A. 1.
35. Ibid., A. 4.

would be an expression of concern for the rights of persons.[36]

The difficulties confronting the idea of restitution arise in the determination of precise compensations for injuries and deprivations, particularly where restitution must involve something more than the return or replacement of external goods. Injury and deprivation take many forms, some of which involve losses that are either irretrievable (as in murder) or incapable of being fully relieved through any compensatory act or acts (as in rape or mutilation). The recognition of the seriousness of such difficulties does not, of course, undermine what is to be said for the moral appropriateness of directing the agencies of *justice* to the rehabilitation of the injured or deprived. Restitution can be virtual where it cannot be actual. The matter is put clearly by St. Thomas:

> Inasmuch as restitution spells a certain repetition, something done over and over again, it supposes an identity of object. And so originally it seems to have been applied mainly to external things . . . which may from one person come to another. But even as the notion of such a division in giving and taking has been transferred from suchlike things to actions and the undergoing of actions, . . . so too the notion of restitution has been extended to dealings which remain in their effects, though not as actual realities. These effects may be physical, as when a body is wounded by a blow, or psychological, as when someone is lastingly defamed or dishonored by opprobrious words.[37]

Concerning restitution as a concept and order of justice, two observations remain to be made. First, the censure of wrongdoing and the compensation for loss can be carried ahead with-

36. The idea of *restitution,* as St. Thomas himself understands, presupposes but is not to be confused with the idea of *distributive justice,* through which the individual has a moral claim upon a fair share of divisible goods, upon access to public goods and services, and upon the guarantees of public safety. Cf. *Summa Theologiae,* Second Part of the Second Part, Q. 61, A. 1, 2.

37. Cf. ibid., Q. 62, A. 1.

out the element of "countersuffering" and, accordingly, without the historic punishments of incarceration, banishment, and death. The argument of Kant, namely, that the principle of retaliation or "countersuffering" is the very meaning of legal justice is unconvincing.[38] What is required in the relations among persons as equals, it would seem, is compensation for injury or loss; and compensation can be exacted of offenders without the application of further punitive measures. Any presumed bearing of punishment upon the deserved suffering of offenders, upon their moral improvement, or upon the deterring of individuals from wrongdoing pertains, one must say, to dominion over human behavior rather than to corrective justice.

In this connection, there is the question whether the absence of stringent punishment, such as incarceration or death, is an invitation to wrongdoing, as the absence of a fence is an invitation to trespassing. It may be argued that if the penalty for injuring another individual is simply the restitution of what the individual has lost, then one can easily bring oneself to harm others knowing that one has the resources, when apprehended and convicted, to restore what St. Thomas calls "the objective balance of things."[39] Indifference to or contempt for what is lawful is doubtless often the case with respect to actions involving penalties such as are imposed for traffic violations and other misdemeanors. And such could conceivably be the case in more serious wrongdoing, including mayhem and murder.

It is important to recognize here the distinction between the character of a wrongdoing and the reason or reasons certain individuals have for behaving or not behaving in such a way. The thought or dread of a penalty is a 'reason' for refraining from injurious action. The *moral* reason for such refraining, of course, is the recognition and acceptance of an act as harmful and wrong. An individual's calculation of his advantage or disadvantage in acting wrongfully, as distinct from his eschewing simply what is intrinsically wrong, belongs to the complex internal transactions bearing upon human volition. There would

38. Kant, *The Metaphysical Elements of Justice*, pp. 100-101.
39. Ibid., pp. 101-2.

be no way for lawmakers to know that the character of a penalty itself will, for any given individual, be decisive in the determination to act or to avoid acting in a wrongful way. It can hardly be said, accordingly, that an individual's ability to pay a fine without financial hardship would in itself make a violation of a traffic regulation more attractive than obeying the law. Just what combination of advantages or what preponderance of advantages over disadvantages would make a traffic violation or theft or mayhem or any other offense attractive to and perhaps compelling for a particular individual is hardly determinable through any general ideas about human motivation and deterrence.

For our second observation, restitution must be taken to embrace offenses that have not been commonly regarded as outrages or crimes. Distinct from injuries that involve consent (e.g., violations of contract) and injuries that do not involve consent (e.g., theft and murder), there are injuries without consent that consist in denials of the access of individuals to certain of the general benefits of organized social life. These are the injuries that consist in and arise from, in J. S. Mill's words, "wretched education, and wretched social conditions." The denial of certain benefits of organized social life is a way of harming other persons, and such harm is no less severe (though perhaps less evident) than direct bodily injury or defamation of character. The severity of such harm is found in effects that involve a chain of disabling consequences affecting the whole life of the individual. As particular injuries to individuals are recognized, those who are directly or indirectly responsible can be identified and required to make restitution. The problems of compensation in such matters are clearly more complex than the problems encountered in the compensation for direct physical and mental harm. The resolution of these problems will demand, accordingly, a largely new development in law and the administration of justice.

Restitution and Responsibility

The acceptance of the idea of restitution requires a modification in some views of responsibility and accountability. Enjoying a long and wide acceptance is the idea that an individual is responsible and must give satisfaction for what he does (or fails to do), if he acts under his own determination, that is, with forethought and without coercion or compulsion of any sort. This view regards every offense as embracing a "subjective element" in the character of a "guilty mind" (*mens rea*). The notion of *mens rea* connects accountability for behavior with *intention to harm* as well as with the harmful act itself. It is what the individual at any moment believed himself to be entering upon, in acting or failing to act, that makes him responsible and accountable for what he does. Intention is simply the determination to involve oneself in a certain doing or line of conduct and in the consequences presumed to follow therefrom. Intention is thus a reflective attention to one's behavior in the effort to support or hinder one condition or another.

There are difficulties in restricting responsibility and accountability to intention. What occurs, together with its consequences, is often not what was intended by an individual; and what was intended, as harmful behavior, often does not result in actual injury to another person. Apart from an individual's own awareness of his intentions, there would seem to be no direct way to discern intention in seeking to determine responsibility for injurious acts. There are, of couse, actions that under certain circumstances are *not* attributable to the individual who "causes" them. Through evidence either before or after the fact (of injurious action), it can be determined that an individual could not have *intended* what he did, by virtue of coercion or insanity or the inability to control his own movements (as in locomotor ataxia), and that he is not accountable for his behavior. Excepting such restrictions upon self-direction, one would be prepared to say that an individual is in control of his actions and is accountable for what he does, whether or not one is prepared to say anything about the individual's intention. That a driver who ran down a pedestrian in a crosswalk intended to inflict injury would perhaps be doubted by most onlookers. Inasmuch as the driver is believed to be in control of his movements (if not of his driving), he would most likely be regarded as *responsible* for the pedestrian's distress.

From the side of the injured individual and the loss sustained by him, it is immaterial whether or not the driver *meant* to harm him. What is apparent is that injury has been sustained and that the driver, as *agent*, failed to avoid what presumably he was capable of avoiding.[40]

The notion of *agency* bridges the gap between intention and consequence in action. In the intention of right action, there is the disposition to support rather than ignore or offend against the rights of others. Although the individual cannot, as Bentham observed, *intend* the *precise* consequences of his acts,[41] the individual does through his agency involve himself in these consequences. It is in this wider sense that one is able to think of action as *voluntary*, that is, not automatic and not constrained by circumstances, and to think of the individual's responsibility for what is voluntary.[42] Thus, under such "strict

40. Cf. H. L. A. Hart, *Punishment and Responsibility. Essays in the Philosophy of Law* (New York: Oxford University Press, 1968), pp. 221-22: "The first question is what general types of outer conduct (*actus reus*) or what sorts of harm are required for liability? The second question is how closely connected with such conduct or such harm must the embodied mind or will of an individual person be to render him liable to punishment? Or, as some would put it, to what extent must the embodied mind or will be the author of the conduct or the harm in order to render him liable? Is it enough that the person made the appropriate bodily movements? Or is it required that he did so when possessed of a certain capacity of control and with a certain knowledge or intention? Or that he caused the harm or stood in some other relationship to it, or to the actual doer of the deed? The legal rules, or parts of legal rules, that answer these various questions define the various forms of connexion which are adequate for liability. . . ."

41. Bentham, *An Introduction to the Principles of Morals and Legislation,* pp. 82-88.

42. Cf. Henry Sidgwick, *The Methods of Ethics,* 7th ed. (Chicago: The University of Chicago Press, 1962), pp. 281-82: ". . . the question arises whether we are bound to make reparation for harm that has been quite blamelessly caused: and it is not easy to answer it decisively. On the whole, I think we should condemn a man who did not offer some reparation for any serious injury caused by him to another—even if quite involuntarily caused, and without negligence: but perhaps we regard this rather as a duty of Benevolence—arising out of the general sympathy that each ought to have for others, intensified by this special occasion—than as a duty of strict justice."

responsibility,"[43] the individual would be expected to answer for injury which he did not intend to bring upon another individual. There is here the idea of responsibility which does not require the idea of guilt and which embraces accountability within what is voluntary without reducing intention to what an individual does as overt behavior.

43. H. L. A. Hart, *Punishment and Responsibility. Essays in the Philosophy of Law,* pp. 176-77.

6 *Epilogue*

Norms of Human Affairs

St. Thomas Aquinas speaks in the *Summa Theologiae* of the tendency in every individual to preserve his own being, to satisfy physical or animal needs, to know the truth, and to live in society without offending others.[1] In taking note of what St. Thomas says, one gives thought to the conditions that would support an individual's expression of these tendencies without frustration and without conflict with other individuals. In a sense the whole of moral philosophy has moved by one path or another to the consideration of the character and possibility of human fulfillment or satisfaction, that is to say, to the consideration of what the individual is able to become.

Moral philosophy, as an investigation of the normative, does not concern itself with the description of human affairs except insofar as the matters described are viewed in relation to determinations that might have been made or that ought to have been made. Clearly the actions of individuals, whether in private concerns or in social relations, do not establish or indicate any *norms* of human life. A norm or measure is not interchangeable with what it measures. It is therefore a mistake to

1. St. Thomas Aquinas, *Summa Theologiae*, First Part of the Second Part, Q. 94, A. 3.

regard as *normative* what is occurring or what has occurred as human practice. *What is done* is always a fact of biography or history; *moral norms,* on the other hand, are matters of intentions and ends. What is done is often contrary to what is found to be fitting or justifiable as one reflects upon one's own affairs or the affairs of others. What is moral is determined at bottom by what is affirmed concerning the best of things or the best of directions to be pursued by any individual or group of individuals. It is seen, accordingly, that one could never come upon a moral norm by merely observing what individuals in fact do or what they are ordered to do.

The attention to describable events may give rise to the illusion that one can treat adequately of human affairs without taking seriously moral affirmations or seeking resolutions of moral disagreements. This illusion has accompanied, in modern times at least, the idea of a 'value-neutral' existence to which moral labels are applied adventitiously according to the tastes or predilections of particular individuals. In a direct way, Hobbes set the stage for the modern posture in his view that human conduct is "caused by the things we see, hear, etc.," that moral ideas reflect simply "the constitution of a man's body in its continual mutation," and that there is no "common rule of good and evil, to be taken from the nature of objects themselves."[2] This general position has been expressed in a somewhat different way in more recent times in the notion of Max Weber that the human sciences cannot provide answers to moral questions. In Weber's words:

> Consider the historical and cultural sciences. They teach us how to understand and interpret political, artistic, literary, and social phenomena in terms of their origins. But they give us no answer to the question, whether the existence of these cultural phenomena have been and are *worth while.* . . . it is one thing to state facts, to determine mathematical or logical relations or the internal structure of cultural values, while it is another thing to answer ques-

2. Thomas Hobbes, *Leviathan,* ed. Michael Oakeshott (Oxford: Basil Blackwell, 1960), chap. 6, p. 32.

> tions of the *value* of culture and its individual contents . . . the various value spheres of the world stand in irreconcilable conflict with each other.[3]

Weber's problem concerning the status of moral values arises from a confusion about human events. It is clear that any *doing* has its time and place in the world of occurrences and, in its precise features and consequences, is observable and distinguishable as is any other occurrence. A *doing*, however, is either *nondeliberate,* as the screaming of an individual who is being subjected to torture, or *deliberate,* as a bystander's leading of a blind person across a busy thoroughfare. Any account of human behavior would be incomplete and distorted if the attention to what is deliberate involved the disregard of what is nondeliberate. Such an account would present human life as a thoroughly reflective enterprise, which of course it is not. At the same time, any account of human behavior that ignores what is deliberate would also be incomplete and distorted and would require the reduction of all valuation to simple affective responses (of pleasure and pain) or to complex responses necessitated by the conditions of cultural existence.

One recognizes that there is a dimension of human behavior that is the proper concern of the moralist, namely, deliberate behavior, and that what is deliberate is purposive and directive in such a way as to affirm the autonomy of the individual as the author of his own affairs. In the phenomena of reflection and choice, there is the causation of moral intelligence or practical wisdom, initiating directions and orderings within the context of the larger world order. It is under the aspect of reflection and choice that human behavior can be thought of as variable in its moral quality and direction, insofar as what is better or worse is taken to be the object of conscious effort. One is able, then, to talk of *moral determinations* (which are expressions of deliberate choice and are corrigible in the light of further thought and judgment) rather than merely of responses and adjustments of

3. Max Weber, "Science as a Vocation," in *From Max Weber: Essays in Sociology,* trans. H. H. Gerth and C. Wright Mills (New York: Oxford University Press, 1958), pp. 145-47.

life to its environment. Physical nature and culture are distinct and often opposed. Culture is to be seen as a moral enterprise, as an order of existence that is devised in accordance with human tendencies and needs and that is modifiable in accordance with the understanding of these tendencies and of ways to their fulfillment.

The Rational Moral Order

In opposing the attack upon morality from the side of mechanism and determinism, one comes to oppose also that attention to moral particularity which undermines the idea of a rational moral order or community. If human practice is not the consequence of inexorable circumstances, then a common morality applicable to all persons and to all organized social life is both thinkable and realizable. Distinct societies can be thought of as carrying forward, under similar or different conditions, the same general program of human good such that an individual's well-being in one society would not differ substantially from another individual's well-being in another society.[4]

The idea of one rational moral order is really entailed in any recognition of a norm distinguishable from the preference of feeling or taste. What is discernible as *fair*, for example, holds for all persons or for all persons in similar situations. Within the broad unity of one moral order there would obtain, of course, that diversity in practice that would be required in meeting the precise needs of individuals and groups under the variable conditions of human existence. There is indeed a richness and significance in the practices that are arrangements or orderings appropriate to different situations. Historical and anthropological accounts provide, in this connection, materials for reflec-

4. Cf. Maurice Merleau-Ponty, *Signs*, trans., with an introduction by Richard C. McCleary (Evanston, Ill.: Northwestern University Press, 1964), p. 124: ". . . in certain complex systems, structures burst apart and . . . become open to 'historical' motivations. Here exchange, symbolic function, and society no longer act as a second nature which is as imperious as the other and effaces it. Each person is invited to define his own system of exchange. By this very process the frontiers between cultures are erased; for the first time, no doubt, a world civilization becomes the order of the day."

tion on the adequacy or suitability of patterns of behavior or modes of life viewed as arising from rational choice and not from biological (racial) or geographical determination.

The rational moral order, embracing both uniformity and diversity of practice, can be thought to be realizable as an alternative to any and all orders that are parochial in character and foundation. In every parochial order, there is a confusion between universality and particularity. A parochial order is one in which the interests of particular individuals or particular groups (ethnic, economic, political, religious) become expressed in terms of the common good and thus take on the guise and sanction of universality. There is the sharpest contrast between the social posture in which particular ends (and means) fall under and are governed by universal ends and the posture in which particular and partisan ends are put forth as having the character and validity of the universal. The rational moral order is simply the system of life resting upon universal or common claims which, as *rights,* determine the range of social policy and the range of corresponding duties.

To talk of rights in a responsible and instructive way is to take on a difficult task in the present-day confusion about the just claims of the individual in society. The difficulty is made all the greater by the overworking of the idea of 'right' through the easy appeal to the validity of claims of all sorts. The affirmation of the 'rights of man' may seem to lose its moral force as declarations become more numerous and more strident. If one comes to believe with Bentham that a right without the power adequate to its exercise is really a nonentity, a mere philosophical fiction, it is but a short step to believe that 'adequate power' is the real ground of right in society and to contend that the advancement of rights is at bottom the pretension of those who have or who seek the resources to promote their own interests and to prevail over others. Every age and every period has its declaration or declarations of rights, which reflect or define alignments of interests—for examples, believer *v.* nonbeliever, lord *v.* serf, master *v.* slave, entrepreneur *v.* worker, skilled worker *v.* unskilled worker.

The notion of *rights,* or *the rights of man,* may be improperly understood or misused for merely partisan concerns. Misunderstanding is a matter both of thought and of language and can be corrected through clarification of meaning and care in the use of a term. Clearly one can avoid the confusion of 'right' as a term indicating a universalizable claim (e.g., the right of free speech, the right to equal pay for equal work) with 'right' as a term indicating a claim of an individual or individuals to a social advantage over others (for example, the presumed right of a landlord to determine unilaterally the rent to be paid by a tenant). Any use of 'right' in the latter sense either lends support to an abuse of an individual's prerogative in society or opens the door to such an abuse.

In addition to the confusion of genuine (i.e., universalizable) with spurious claims, there is the confusion related to the idea of genuine claims as determinations or dispensations of political society. On this view, articulated by Edmund Burke, the "real rights" of individuals are *political rights* obtaining as compromises between liberty and restraint. In Burke's words:

> The pretended rights of . . . theorists are all extremes; and in proportion as they are metaphysically true they are morally and politically false. . . . The rights of men in governments are their advantages, and these are often in balances between differences of good, in compromizes between good and evil, and sometimes between evil and evil. Political reason is a computing principle. . . .[5]

The "computing principle" to which Burke appeals does not really supply what is needed to make his notion of political rights tenable. If indeed political affairs are concerned with "restraints and liberties," then there must be a principle of equality or fairness that is the rational and moral guide in all practical determinations and that is therefore anterior to such determinations. One considers also that among the rights of persons there would clearly be the right of an individual to the advantages of organized social life. This right obviously cannot

5. Edmund Burke, *Reflections on the Revolution in France*, ed. Thomas H. D. Mahoney (Indianapolis: The Bobbs-Merrill Company, Inc., 1975), p. 75.

itself be political in origin, for the right *to* political society and to the benefits of a just political order cannot be derived *from* political society.

It would seem that the rights with which one is concerned in ethics and politics are not "political rights" but the rights of persons in political society. It is apparent that the interests of persons in any society are complex and variable and that new demands continue to be advanced as claims to be satisfied in accomplishing the purposes of individuals and their groups. There is a contest of demands in every society as some claims are declared to be more real than others. In this contest, *means* often come to be confused with *ends* as the devices of the advocacy of interests are taken to establish the propriety of these interests. If one approaches the propriety of interests from the side of *advocacy,* one simply encounters antinomies of interests to which no scheme of equity is applicable. If, however, one approaches interests and their propriety from the side of the *claims of persons,* one can think of an order of reciprocal freedom under which it is *fair* for an individual to demand as a citizen only what others have an equal chance to enjoy according to their need.

Considering the antinomies of interests in the contemporary world, the whole notion of human rights may appear to contribute more to social confusion and disruption than to the freedom of the individual and the preservation of the common good. What is clearly essential, it would seem, is the recognition of a moral order under which any *right* of one person is thought of as coexisting in idea and in exercise with the rights of all other persons. A right *in idea* is at once both personal and social; it is a thing of limit as well as of liberty. In its foundation in the status of the individual as a person, a right is a universalizable claim. And it is from this moral side that an individual, concerned with his own interests and claims, can see or can be persuaded to see that what is fair can never give one individual a social advantage over another. The individual's well-being can be thought of and promoted without translating interests into unilateral advantages or seeking to preserve such unilateral advantages as already exist. Under the notion of human rights, the attention in the treatment of political society and law shifts from the realities of power and influence to the demands of justicc.

The idea of a rational moral order embraces the notion of law as rational governance that makes explicit the rights and duties of free persons. Law is the common authority of free individuals who, in their role as citizens, impose upon themselves that order which is both expressive and protective of their freedom. Law in its very idea as rational governance expresses what is just and fair. Law simply publishes and enforces what morality requires. Contrary to this view of law (as governance in accordance with morality) is the view that law is other than morality and that law in its autonomy establishes its own domain of commands, precedents, sanctions, threats, and penalties. Obviously, such separation of law from morality cannot be maintained. The 'law' which is presumably free of morality imposes its own 'morality' in ordering that certain ends are to be promoted by definite means and in instituting, with open or furtive borrowing from moral discourse, what is to be accepted concerning the meaning of justice, obedience, fault or wrongdoing, guilt, and punishment. It is only the pretension to autonomy that gives rise to the illusion that the law is beyond moral scrutiny and that it is meaningless to talk of an unjust law.

If the affirmation of reciprocal freedom is the foundation of civil society, then the guarantee of freedom is the foundation of law. And if one can speak meaningfully of injustice as the denial of freedom, then one can speak meaningfully of unjust law as the public expression of such denial. Justice itself stands forth as a moral norm to be observed evenly in the law, whether in the correction of wrongdoing or the distribution of goods and services, in the protection of civil liberties or the preservation of safety and peace.

Selected Bibliography

Aristotle. *Nicomachean Ethics.* Translated by H. Rackham. Cambridge, Mass.: Harvard University Press, 1975.

——. *Politics.* Translated by H. Rackham. Cambridge, Mass.: Harvard University Press, 1972.

Austin, John. *The Province of Jurisprudence Determined.* In *Lectures on Jurisprudence.* London: John Murray, 1873.

Beccaria, Cesare. *On Crimes and Punishments.* Translated by Henry Paolucci. Indianapolis: The Bobbs-Merrill Company, Inc., 1963.

Bentham, Jeremy. *A Fragment on Government.* Edited by F. C. Montague. London: Oxford University Press, 1951.

——. *An Introduction to the Principles of Morals and Legislation.* New York: Hafner Publishing Company, 1948.

Bergson, Henri. *The Two Sources of Morality and Religion.* New York: Henry Holt and Company, 1935.

Blackstone, William. *Commentaries on the Laws of England.* Edited by St. George Tucker. South Hackensack, N.J.: Rothman Reprints, 1969.

Bosanquet, Bernard. *The Philosophical Theory of the State.* London: Macmillan and Company, Ltd., 1965.

Bradley, F. H. *Essays in Truth and Reality.* Oxford: The Clarendon Press, 1968.

Buchland, W. W. *Some Reflections on Jurisprudence.* Cambridge: Cambridge University Press, 1945.

Butler, Joseph. *Sermons on Human Nature.* In *Modern British Moralists,* edited by L. A. Selby-Bigge. Indianapolis: The Bobbs-Merrill

Company, Inc., 1964.
Cairns, Huntington. *Legal Philosophy from Plato to Hegel.* Baltimore: The Johns Hopkins Press, 1966.
Cardozo, Benjamin. *The Growth of the Law.* New Haven: Yale University Press, 1924.
——. *The Nature of the Judicial Process.* New Haven: Yale University Press, 1921.
Cohen, Morris R. *Law and the Social Order. Essays in Legal Philosophy.* Westport, Conn.: Greenwood Press, 1972.
——. *Reason and Law.* Glencoe, Ill.: Free Press, 1950.
Ewing, A. C. *The Morality of Punishment.* Montclair, N.J.: Patterson Smith, 1970.
Friedmann, Wolfgang. *Law in a Changing Society.* Berkeley and Los Angeles: University of California Press, 1959.
——. *Legal Theory.* 5th ed. London: Stevens, 1967.
Friedrich, Carl Joachim. *The Philosophy of Law in Historical Perspective.* Chicago: The University of Chicago Press, 1958.
Fuller, Lon. *The Law in Quest of Itself.* Chicago: The Foundation Press, 1940.
——. *The Morality of Law.* Rev. ed. New Haven: Yale University Press, 1969.
Gény, François. *Science et technique en droit privé positif.* Paris: Société du Recueil Sivey, 1921-30.
Gierke, Otto. *Natural Law and the Theory of Society, 1500 to 1800.* Translated by Ernest Barker. Boston: Beacon Press, 1957.
Green, T. H. *Prolegomena to Ethics.* Edited by A. C. Bradley. 5th ed. Oxford: The Clarendon Press, 1907.
Hare, R. M. *Freedom and Reason.* Oxford: The Clarendon Press, 1963.
——. *The Language of Morals.* Oxford: The Clarendon Press, 1952.
Hart, H. L. A. *The Concept of Law.* Oxford: The Clarendon Press, 1962.
——. *Responsibility and Punishment. Essays in the Philosophy of Law.* New York: Oxford University Press, 1968.
Hegel, G. W. F. *Philosophy of Right.* Translated by T. M. Knox. Oxford: The Clarendon Press, 1962.
Hobbes, Thomas. *Leviathan.* Edited by Michael Oakeshott. Oxford: Basil Blackwell, 1960.
Hooker, Richard. *Of the Laws of Ecclesiastical Polity.* London: J. M. Dent and Sons, Ltd. 1954.
Hume, David. *An Enquiry Concerning the Principles of Morals.* Edited by L. A. Selby-Bigge. Revised by P. H. Nidditch. Oxford: The Clarendon Press, 1975.
——. *A Treatise of Human Nature.* Edited by L. A. Selby-Bigge. Oxford: The Clarendon Press, 1958.
Kant, Immanuel. *Metaphysics of Morals: The Doctrine of Virtue.* Trans-

lated by Mary J. Gregor. New York: Harper and Row, Publishers, 1964.

——. *Metaphysics of Morals: The Metaphysical Elements of Justice.* Translated by John Ladd. Indianapolis: The Bobbs-Merrill Company, Inc., 1964.

Kelsen, Hans. *General Theory of Law and State.* Translated by Anders Wedberg. New York: Russell and Russell, 1961.

——. *Reine Rechtslehre.* 2d ed. Vienna: F. Deuticke, 1960.

Llewellyn, Karl N. *The Bramble Bush.* New York: Oceana Publications, 1951.

Locke, John. *The Second Treatise of Civil Government.* Edited by J. W. Gough. Oxford: Basil Blackwell, 1948.

McIlwain, Charles H. *The Growth of Political Thought in the West.* New York: The Macmillan Company, 1955.

Merryman, John Henry. *The Civil Law Tradition.* Stanford: Stanford University Press, 1969.

Mill, J. S. *Utilitarianism.* In *The Utilitarians.* Garden City, N.Y.: Dolphin Books, 1961.

Moore, G. E. *Principia Ethica.* Cambridge: Cambridge University Press, 1954.

Passarin d'Entrèves, A. *The Medieval Contribution to Political Thought.* London: Oxford University Press, 1939.

——. *Natural Law. An Introduction to Legal Philosophy.* London: Hutchinson's University Library, 1955.

Perelman, Chaim. *The Idea of Justice and the Problem of Argument.* Translated by J. Petrie. London: Routledge and Kegan Paul, Ltd., 1963.

Perry, R. B. *The Realms of Value.* Cambridge, Mass.: Harvard University Press, 1954.

Plato. *Republic.* Translated by Paul Shorey. Cambridge, Mass.: Harvard University Press, 1963.

Plucknett, T. F. T. *A Concise History of the Common Law.* 5th ed. Boston: Little, Brown, and Company, 1956.

Pollock, Frederick. *Essays in the Law.* Hamden, Conn.: Archon Books, 1969.

Popper, Karl. *The Open Society and Its Enemies.* 5th ed., rev. London: Routledge and Kegan Paul, Ltd., 1966.

Pound, Roscoe. *An Introduction to the Philosophy of Law.* New Haven: Yale University Press, 1922.

Price, Richard. *A Review of the Principal Questions in Morals.* In *British Moralists,* edited by L. A. Selby-Bigge. Indianapolis: The Bobbs-Merrill Company, Inc., 1964.

Prichard, H. A. *Moral Obligation. Essays and Lectures.* Oxford: The Clarendon Press, 1949.

Radbruch, Gustav. *Rechtsphilosophie*. 6th ed. Stuttgart: K. F. Koehler, 1963.

Rawls, John. *A Theory of Justice*. Cambridge, Mass.: Harvard University Press, 1971.

Savigny, F. K. von. *Geschichte des römischen Rechts im Mittelalter*. Darmstadt: Gentner, 1956.

Sidgwick, Henry. *The Methods of Ethics*. 7th ed. Chicago: The University of Chicago Press, 1962.

Stammler, Rudolf. *The Theory of Justice*. Translated by Isaac Husik. New York: The Macmillan Company, 1925.

Strauss, Leo. *Natural Right and History*. Chicago: The University of Chicago Press, 1953.

Thomas Aquinas, Saint. *Summa Theologiae*. Translated by Blackfriars. London: Eyre and Spottiswoode, 1964.

Veatch, Henry B. *For An Ontology of Morals. A Critique of Contemporary Ethical Theory*. Evanston: Northwestern University Press, 1971.

Vinogradoff, Paul. *Common Sense in Law*. New York: Henry Holt and Company, 1914.

——. *Custom and Right*. Cambridge, Mass.: Harvard University Press, 1925.

Wild, John. *Plato's Modern Enemies and the Theory of Natural Law*. Chicago: The University of Chicago Press, 1953.

Wootton, Barbara. *Crime and the Criminal Law*. London: Stevens, 1963.

Wright, Georg Henrik von. *Norm and Action. A Logical Inquiry*. London: Routledge and Kegan Paul, Ltd., 1963.

——. *The Varieties of Goodness*. London: Routledge and Kegan Paul, Ltd., 1963.

Index of Names

Index of Subjects